The Story of the

by James Mark Baldwin

PREFACE.

In this little book I have endeavoured to maintain the simplicity which is the ideal of this series. It is more difficult, however, to be simple in a topic which, even in its illustrations, demands of the reader more or less facility in the exploration of his own mind. I am persuaded that the attempt to make the matter of psychology more elementary than is here done, would only result in making it untrue and so in defeating its own object.

In preparing the book I have secured the right and welcomed the opportunity to include certain more popular passages from earlier books and articles. It is necessary to say this, for some people are loath to see a man repeat himself. When one has once said a thing, however, about as well as he can say it, there is no good reason that he should be forced into the pretence of saying something different simply to avoid using the same form of words a second time. The question, of course, is as to whether he should not then resign himself to keeping still, and letting others do the further speaking. There is much to be said for such a course. But if one have the right to print more severe and difficult things, and think he really has something to say which would instruct the larger audience, it would seem only fair to allow him to speak in the simpler way also, even though all that he says may not have the merit of escaping the charge of infringing his own copyrights!

I am indebted to the proprietors of the following magazines for the use of such passages: The Popular Science Monthly, The Century Magazine, The Inland Educator; and with them I also wish to thank The Macmillan Company and the owners of Appletons' Universal Cyclop鎰 ia.

As to the scope and contents of the Story, I have aimed to include enough statement of methods and results in each of the great departments of psychological research to give the reader an intelligent idea of what is being done, and to whet his appetite for more detailed information. In the choice of materials I have relied frankly on my own experience and in debatable matters given my own opinions. This gives greater reality to the several topics, besides making it possible, by this general statement, at once to acknowledge it, and also to avoid discussion and citation of authorities in the text. At the same time, in the exposition of general principles I have endeavoured to keep well within the accepted truth and terminology of psychology.

It will be remarked that in several passages the evolution theory is adopted in its application to the mind. While this great theory can not be discussed in these pages, yet I may say that, in my opinion, the evidence in favour of it is about the same, and about as strong, as in biology, where it is now made a presupposition of scientific explanation. So far from being unwelcome, I find it in psychology no less than in biology a great gain, both from the point of view of scientific knowledge and from that of philosophical theory. Every great law that is added to our store adds also to our conviction that the universe is run through with Mind. Even so-called Chance, which used to be the "bogie" behind Natural Selection, has now been found to illustrate--in the law of Probabilities--the absence of Chance. As Professor Pearson has said: "We recognise that our conception of Chance is now utterly different from that of yore.... What we are to understand by a chance distribution is one in accordance with law, and one the nature of which can, for all practical purposes, be closely predicted." If the universe be pregnant with purpose, as we all wish to believe, why should not this purpose work itself out by an evolution process under law?--and if under law, why not the law of Probabilities? We who have our lives insured provide for our children through our knowledge and use of this law; and our plans for their welfare, in most of the affairs of life, are based upon the recognition of it. Who will deny to the Great Purpose a similar resource in producing the universe and in providing for us all?

I add in a concluding section on Literature some references to various books in English, classified under the headings of the chapters of the text. These works will further enlighten the reader, and, if he persevere, possibly make a psychologist of him.

J. MARK BALDWIN.

PRINCETON, April, 1898.

CONTENTS.

THE STORY OF THE MIND

CHAPTER I.

THE SCIENCE OF THE MIND--PSYCHOLOGY,

Psychology is the science of the mind. It aims to find out all about the mind--
the whole story--just as the other sciences aim to find out all about the
subjects of which they treat--astronomy, of the stars; geology, of the earth;
physiology, of the body. And when we wish to trace out the story of the mind,
as psychology has done it, we find that there are certain general truths with
which we should first acquaint ourselves; truths which the science has been a
very long time finding out, but which we can now realize without a great deal
of explanation. These general truths, we may say, are preliminary to the story
itself; they deal rather with the need of defining, first of all, the subject or
topic of which the story is to be told.

1. The first such truth is that the mind is not the possession of man alone.
Other creatures have minds. Psychology no longer confines itself, as it
formerly did, to the human soul, denying to the animals a place in this highest
of all the sciences. It finds itself unable to require any test or evidence of the
presence of mind which the animals do not meet, nor does it find any place at
which the story of the mind can begin higher up than the very beginnings of
life. For as soon as we ask, "How much mind is necessary to start with?" we
have to answer, "Any mind at all"; and all the animals are possessed of some
of the actions which we associate with mind. Of course, the ascertainment of
the truth of this belongs--as the ascertainment of all the truths of nature
belongs--to scientific investigation itself. It is the scientific man's rule not to
assume anything except as he finds facts to support the assumption. So we
find a great department of psychology devoted to just this question--i.e., of
tracing mind in the animals and in the child, and noting the stages of what is
called its "evolution" in the ascending scale of animal life, and its
"development" in the rapid growth which every child goes through in the
nursery. This gives us two chapters of the story of the mind. Together they
are called "Genetic Psychology," having two divisions, "Animal or
Comparative Psychology" and "Child Psychology."

2. Another general truth to note at the outset is this: that we are able to get

real knowledge about the mind. This may seem at first sight a useless question to raise, seeing that our minds are, in the thought of many, about the only things we are really sure of. But that sort of sureness is not what science seeks. Every science requires some means of investigation, some method of procedure, which is more exact than the mere say-so of common sense; and which can be used over and again by different investigators and under different conditions. This gives a high degree of verification and control to the results once obtained. The chemist has his acids, and reagents, and blowpipes, etc.; they constitute his instruments, and by using them, under certain constant rules, he keeps to a consistent method. So with the physiologist; he has his microscope, his staining fluids, his means of stimulating the tissues of the body, etc. The physicist also makes much of his lenses, and membranes, and electrical batteries, and X-ray apparatus. In like manner it is necessary that the psychologist should have a recognised way of investigating the mind, which he can lay before anybody saying: "There, you see my results, you can get them for yourself by the same method that I used."

In fulfilling this requirement the psychologist resorts to two methods of procedure. He is able to investigate the mind in two ways, which are of such general application that anybody of sufficient training to make scientific observations at all can repeat them and so confirm the results. One of these is what is called Introspection. It consists in taking note of one's own mind, as all sorts of changes are produced in it, such as emotions, memories, associations of events now gone, etc., and describing everything that takes place. Other persons can repeat the observations with their own minds, and see that what the first reports is true. This results in a body of knowledge which is put together and called "Introspective Psychology," and one chapter of the story should be devoted to that.

Then the other way we have is that of experimenting on some one else's mind. We can act on our friends and neighbours in various ways, making them feel, think, accept, refuse this and that, and then observe how they act. The differences in their action will show the differences in the feelings, etc., which we have produced. In pursuing this method the psychologist takes a person--called the "subject" or the "re-agent"--into his laboratory, asks him to be willing to follow certain directions carefully, such as holding an electric handle, blowing into a tube, pushing a button, etc., when he feels, sees, or hears certain things; this done with sufficient care, the results are found recorded in certain ways which the psychologist has arranged beforehand. This second way of proceeding gives results which are gathered under the two headings "Experimental" and "Physiological Psychology." They should also have chapters in our story.

3. There is besides another truth which the psychologist nowadays finds very fruitful for his knowledge of the mind; this is the fact that minds vary much in different individuals, or classes of individuals. First, there is the pronounced difference between healthy minds and diseased minds. The differences are so great that we have to pursue practically different methods of treating the diseased, not only as a class apart from the well minds-- putting such diseased persons into institutions--but also as differing from one another. Just as the different forms of bodily disease teach us a great deal about the body--its degree of strength, its forms of organization and function, its limitations, its heredity, the inter-connection of its parts, etc.--so mental diseases teach us much about the normal mind. This gives another sphere of information which constitutes "Abnormal Psychology" or "Mental Pathology."

There are also very striking variations between individuals even within normal life; well people are very different from one another. All that is commonly meant by character or temperament as distinguishing one person from another is evidence of these differences. But really to know all about mind we should see what its variations are, and endeavour to find out why the variations exist. This gives, then, another topic, "Individual or Variational Psychology." This subject should also have notice in the story.

4. Allied with this the demand is made upon the psychologist that he show to the teacher how to train the mind; how to secure its development in the individual most healthfully and productively, and with it all in a way to allow the variations of endowment which individuals show each to bear its ripest fruit. This is "Educational or Pedagogical Psychology."

5. Besides all these great undertakings of the psychologist, there is another department of fact which he must some time find very fruitful, although as yet he has not been able to investigate it thoroughly: he should ask about the place of the mind in the world at large. If we seek to know what the mind has done in the world, what a wealth of story comes to us from the very

beginnings of history! Mind has done all that has been done: it has built human institutions, indited literature, made science, discovered the laws of Nature, used the forces of the material world, embodied itself in all the monuments which stand to testify to the presence of man. What could tell us more of what mind is than this record of what mind has done? The ethnologists are patiently tracing the records left by early man in his utensils, weapons, clothing, religious rites, architectural remains, etc., and the anthropologists are seeking to distinguish the general and essential from the accidental and temporary in all the history of culture and civilization. They are making progress very slowly, and it is only here and there that principles are being discovered which reveal to the psychologist the necessary modes of action and development of the mind. All this comes under the head of "Race Psychology."

6. Finally, another department, the newest of all, investigates the action of minds when they are thrown together in crowds. The animals herd, the insects swarm, most creatures live in companies; they are gregarious, and man no less is social in his nature. So there is a psychology of herds, crowds, mobs, etc., all put under the heading of "Social Psychology." It asks the question, What new phases of the mind do we find when individuals unite in common action?--or, on the other hand, when they are artificially separated?

We now have with all this a fairly complete idea of what The Story of the Mind should include, when it is all told. Many men are spending their lives each at one or two of these great questions. But it is only as the results are all brought together in a consistent view of that wonderful thing, the mind, that we may hope to find out all that it is. We must think of it as a growing, developing thing, showing its stages of evolution in the ascending animal scale, and also in the unfolding of the child; as revealing its nature in every change of our daily lives which we experience and tell to one another or find ourselves unable to tell; as allowing itself to be discovered in the laboratory, and as willing to leave the marks of its activity on the scientist's blackened drum and the dial of the chronoscope; as subject to the limitations of health and disease, needing to be handled with all the resources of the asylum, the reformatory, the jail, as well as with the delicacy needed to rear the sensitive girl or to win the love of the bashful maid; as manifesting itself in the development of humanity from the first rude contrivances for the use of fire, the first organizations for defence, and the first inscriptions of picture writing, up to the modern inventions in electricity, the complex constitutions of government, and the classic productions of literary art; and as revealing its possibilities finally in the brutal acts of the mob, the crimes of a lynching party, and the deeds of collective righteousness performed by our humane and religious societies.

It would be impossible, of course, within the limits of this little volume, to give even the main results in so many great chapters of this ambitious and growing science. I shall not attempt that; but the rather select from the various departments certain outstanding results and principles. From these as elevations the reader may see the mountains on the horizon, so to speak, which at his leisure, and with better guides, he may explore. The choice of materials from so rich a store has depended also, as the preface states, on the writer's individual judgment, and it is quite probable that no one will find the matters altogether wisely chosen. All the great departments now thus briefly described, however, are represented in the following chapters.

CHAPTER II.

WHAT OUR MINDS HAVE IN COMMON--INTROSPECTIVE PSYCHOLOGY.

Of all the sources now indicated from which the psychologist may draw, that of so-called Introspective Psychology--the actual reports of what we find going on in our minds from time to time--is the most important. This is true for two great reasons, which make Psychology different from all the other sciences. The first claim which the introspective method has upon us arises from the fact that it is only by it that we can examine the mind directly, and get its events in their purity. Each of us knows himself better than he knows any one else. So this department, in which we deal each with his own consciousness at first hand, is more reliable, if free from error, than any of those spheres in which we examine other persons, so long as we are dealing with the psychology of the individual. The second reason that this method of procedure is most important is found in the fact that all the other departments of psychology--and with them all the other sciences--have to use introspection, after all, to make sure of the results which they get by other methods. For example, the natural scientist, the botanist, let us say, and the physical scientist, the electrician, say, can not observe the plants or the electric sparks without really using his introspection upon what is before him. The light from the plant has to go into his brain and leave a certain effect in his mind, and then he has to use introspection to report what he sees. The astronomer who has bad eyes can not observe the stars well or discover the facts about them, because his introspection in reporting what he sees proceeds on the imperfect and distorted images coming in from his defective eyesight. So a man given to exaggeration, who is not able to report truthfully what he remembers, can not be a good botanist, since this defect in introspection will render his observation of the plants unreliable.

In practice the introspective method has been most important, and the development of psychology has been up to very recently mainly due to its use. As a consequence, there are many general principles of mental action and many laws of mental growth already discovered which should in the first instance engage our attention. They constitute the main framework of the building; and we should master them well before we go on to find the various applications which they have in the other departments of the subject.

The greater results of "Introspective" or, as it is very often called, "General" psychology may be summed up in a few leading principles, which sound more or less abstract and difficult, but which will have many concrete illustrations in the subsequent chapters. The facts of experience, the actual events which we find taking place in our minds, fall naturally into certain great divisions. These are very easily distinguished from one another. The first distinction is covered by the popularly recognised difference between "thought and conduct," or "knowledge and life." On the one hand, the mind is looked at as receiving, taking in, learning; and on the other hand, as acting, willing, doing this or that. Another great distinction contrasts a third mental condition, "feeling," with both of the other two. We say a man has knowledge, but little feeling, head but no heart; or that he knows and feels the right but does not live up to it.

I. On the side of Reception we may first point out the avenues through which our experiences come to us: these are the senses--a great number, not simply the five special senses of which we were taught in our childhood. Besides Sight, Hearing, Taste, Smell, and Touch, we now know of certain others very definitely. There are Muscle sensations coming from the moving of our limbs, Organic sensations from the inner vital organs, Heat and Cold sensations which are no doubt distinct from each other, Pain sensations probably having their own physical apparatus, sensations from the Joints, sensations of Pressure, of Equilibrium of the body, and a host of peculiar sensational conditions which, for all we know, may be separate and distinct, or may arise from combinations of some of the others. Such, for example, are the sensations which are felt when a current of electricity is sent through the arm.

All these give the mind its material to work upon; and it gets no material in the first instance from any other source. All the things we know, all our opinions, knowledges, beliefs, are absolutely dependent at the start upon this supply of material from our senses; although, as we shall see, the mind gets a long way from its first subjection to this avalanche of sensations which come constantly pouring in upon it from the external world. Yet this is the essential and capital function of Sensation: to supply the material on which the mind does the work in its subsequent thought and action.

Next comes the process by which the mind holds its material for future use, the process of Memory; and with it the process by which it combines its material together in various useful forms, making up things and persons out of the material which has been received and remembered--called Association of Ideas, Thinking, Reasoning, etc. All these processes used to be considered as separate "faculties" of the soul and as showing the mind doing different things. But that view is now completely given up. Psychology now treats the activity of the mind in a much more simple way. It says: Mind does only one thing; in all these so-called faculties we have the mind doing this one thing only on the different materials which come and go in it. This one thing is the combining, or holding together, of the elements which first come to it as sensations, so that it can act on a group of them as if they were only one and represented only one external thing. Let me illustrate this single and peculiar sort of process as it goes on in the mind.

We may ask how the child apprehends an orange out there on the table before him. It can not be said that the orange goes into the child's mind by any one of its senses. By sight he gets only the colour and shape of the orange, by smell he gets only its odour, by taste its sweetness, and by touch its smoothness, rotundity, etc. Furthermore, by none of these senses does he find out the individuality of the orange, or distinguish it from other things which involve the same or similar sensations--say an apple. It is easy to see that after each of the senses has sent in its report something more is necessary: the combining of them all together in the same place and at the same time, the bringing up of an appropriate name, and with that a sort of relating or distinguishing of this group of sensations from those of the apple. Only then can we say that the knowledge, "here is an orange," has been reached. Now this is the one typical way the mind has of acting, this combining of all the items or groups of items into ever larger and more fruitful combinations. This is called Apperception. The mind, we say, "apperceives" the orange when it is able to treat all the separate sensations together as standing for one thing. And the various circumstances under which the mind does this give the occasions for the different names which the earlier psychology used for marking off different "faculties."

These names are still convenient, however, and it may serve to make the subject clear, as well as to inform the reader of the meaning of these terms, to show how they all refer to this one kind of mental action.

The case of the orange illustrates what is usually called Perception. It is the case in which the result is the knowledge of an actual object in the outside world. When the same process goes on after the actual object has been removed it is Memory. When it goes on again in a way which is not controlled by reference to such an outside object--usually it is a little fantastic, as in dreams or fancy, but often it is useful as being so well done as to anticipate what is really true in the outside world--then it is Imagination. If it is actually untrue, but still believed in, we call it Illusion or Hallucination. When it uses mere symbols, such as words, gestures, writing, etc., to stand for whole groups of things, it is Thinking or Reasoning. So we may say that what the mind arrives at through this its one great way of acting, no matter which of these forms it takes on, except in the cases in which it is not true in its results to the realities, is Knowledge.

Thus we see that the terms and faculties of the older psychology can be arranged under this doctrine of Apperception without the necessity of thinking of the mind as doing more than the one thing. It simply groups and combines its material in different ways and in ever higher degrees of complexity.

Apperception, then, is the one principle of mental activity on the side of its reception and treatment of the materials of experience.

There is another term very current in psychology by which this same process is sometimes indicated: the phrase Association of Ideas. This designates the fact that when two things have been perceived or thought of together, they tend to come up together in the mind in the future; and when a thing has been perceived which resembles another, or is contrasted with it, they tend to recall each other in the same way. It is plain, however, that this phrase is applied to the single thoughts, sensations, or other mental materials, in their relations or connections among themselves. They are said to be "associated" with one another. This way of speaking of the mental materials, instead of speaking of the mind's activity, is convenient; and it is quite right to do so, since it is no contradiction to say that the thoughts, etc., which the mind "apperceives" remain "associated" together. From this explanation it is evident that the Association of Ideas also comes under the mental process of Apperception of which we have been speaking.

There is, however, another tendency of the mind in the treatment of its material, a tendency which shows us in actual operation the activity with which we have now become familiar. When we come to look at any particular case of apperception or association we find that the process must go on from the platform which the mind's attainments have already reached. The passing of the mental states has been likened to a stream which flows on from moment to moment with no breaks. It is so continuous that we can never say: "I will start afresh, forget the past, and be uninfluenced by my history." However we may wish this, we can never do it; for the oncoming current of the stream is just what we speak of as ourselves, and we can not avoid bringing the memories, imaginations, expectations, disappointments, etc., up to the present. So the effect which any new event or experience, happening for the first time, is to have upon us depends upon the way it fits into the current of these onflowing influences. The man I see for the first time may be so neutral to me that I pass him unregarded. But let him return after I have once remarked him, or let him resemble a man whom I know, or let him give me some reason to observe, fear, revere, think of him in any way, then he is a positive factor in my stream. He has been taken up into the flow of my mental life, and he henceforth contributes something to it.

For example, a little child, after learning to draw a man's face, with two eyes, the nose and mouth, and one ear on each side, will afterward, when told to draw a profile, still put in two eyes and affix an ear to each side. The drift of mental habit tells on the new result and he can not escape it.

He will still put in the two eyes and two ears when he has before him a copy showing only one ear and neither eye.

In all such cases the new is said to be Assimilated to the old. The customary figure for man in the child's memory assimilates the materials of the new copy set before him.

Now this tendency is universal. The mind must assimilate its new material as much as possible, thus making the old stand for the new. Otherwise there would be no containing the fragmentary details which we should have to remember and handle. Furthermore, it is through this tendency that we go on to form the great classes of objects--such as man, animal, virtue--into which numbers of similar details are put, and which we call General Notions or Concepts.

We may understand by Assimilation, therefore, the general tendency of new experiences to be treated by us in the ways which similar material has been treated before, with the result that the mind proceeds from the particular case to the general class.

Summing up our outcome so far, we find that general psychology has reached three great principles in its investigation of knowledge. First, we have the combining tendency of the mind, the grouping together and relating of mental states and of things, called Apperception. Then, second, there are the particular relations established among the various states, etc., which are combined; these are called Associations of Ideas. And, third, there is the tendency of the mind to use its old experiences and habits as general patterns or nets for the sorting out and distributing of all the new details of daily life; this is called Assimilation.

II. Let us now turn to the second great aspect of the mind, as general or introspective psychology considers it, the aspect which presents itself in Action or conduct. The fact that we act is of course as important as the fact that we think or the fact that we feel; and the distinction which separates thought and action should not be made too sharp.

Yet there is a distinction. To understand action we must again go to introspection. This comes out as soon as we ask how we reach our knowledge of the actions of others. Of course, we say at once that we see them. And that is true; we do see them, while as to their thoughts we only infer them from what we see of their action. But, on the other hand, we may ask: How do we come to infer this or that thought from this or that action of another? The only reply is: Because when we act in the same way this is the way we feel. So we get back in any case to our own consciousness and must ask how is this action related to this thought in our own mind.

To this question psychology has now a general answer: Our action is always the result of our thought, of the elements of knowledge which are at the time present in the mind. Of course, there are actions which we do from purely nervous reasons. These are the Instincts, which come up again when we consider the animals. But these we may neglect so long as we are investigating actions which we consider our own. Apart from the Instincts, the principle holds that behind every action which our conduct shows there must be something thought of, some sensation or knowledge then in mind, some feeling swelling within our breast, which prompts to the action.

This general principle is Motor Suggestion. It simply means that we are unable to have any thought or feeling whatever, whether it comes from the senses, from memory, from the words, conduct, or command of others, which does not have a direct influence upon our conduct. We are quite unable to avoid the influence of our own thoughts upon our conduct, and often the most trivial occurrences of our daily lives act as suggestions to deeds of very great importance to ourselves and others. For example, the influence of the newspaper reports of crime stimulate other individuals to perform the same crimes by this principle of suggestion; for the fact is that the reading of the report causes us to entertain the thoughts, and these thoughts tend to arouse in us their corresponding trains of suggested action.

The most interesting and striking sphere of operation of the principle of Suggestion (of other sorts as well as motor) is what is commonly known simply as Hypnotism. To that, as well as to further illustrations of Suggestion, we will return later on.

We are able, however, to see a little more in detail how the law of Motor Suggestion works by asking what sort of action is prompted in each case of thought or feeling, at the different levels of the mind's activity which have been distinguished above as all illustrating Apperception--e.g., the stages known as Perception, Imagination, Reasoning, etc.

We act, of course, on our perceptions constantly; most of our routine life is made up of such action on the perceptions of objects which lie about us. The positions of things in the house, in the streets, in the office, in the store, are so well known that we carry out a series of actions with reference to these objects without much supervision from our consciousness. Here the law of Motor Suggestion works along under the guidance of Perception, Memory, and the Association of Ideas. Then we find also, in much of our action, an element due to the exercise of the Imagination. We fill in the gaps in the world of perception by imagining appropriate connections; and we then act as if we knew that these imaginations were realities. This is especially true in our intercourse with our fellow-men. We never really know what they will do from time to time. Their action is still future and uncertain; but from our familiarity with their character, we surmise or imagine what they expect or think, and we then act so as to make our conduct fit into theirs. Here is suggestion of a personal kind which depends upon our ability, in a sense, to reconstruct the character of others, leading us out into appropriate action. This is the sphere of the most important affairs of our lives. It appears especially so when we consider its connection with the next great sort of action from suggestion.

This next and highest sphere is action from the general or abstract thoughts which we have been able to work up by the apperceiving activity of the mind. In this sphere we have a special name for those thoughts which influence us directly and lead us to action: we call such thoughts Motives. We also have a special name for the sort of action which is prompted by clearly-thought-out motives: Will. But in spite of this emphasis given to certain actions of ours as springing from what is called Will, we must be careful to see that Will is not a new faculty, or capacity, added to mind, and which is different from the ways of action which the mind had before the Will arose. Will is only a name for the action upon suggestions of conduct which are so clear in our minds that we are able to deliberate upon them, acting only after some reflection, and so having a sense that the action springs from our own choice. The real reasons for action, however, are thoughts, in this case, just as in the earlier cases they were. In this case we call them Motives; but we are dependent upon these Motives, these Suggestions; we can not act without Motives, nor can we fail to act on those Motives which we have; just as, in the earlier cases, we could not act without some sort of Perceptions or Imaginations or Memories, and we could not fail to act on the Perceptions or other mental states which we had. Voluntary action or Will is therefore only a complex and very highly conscious case of the general law of Motor Suggestion; it is the form which suggested action takes on when Apperception is at its highest level.

The converse of Suggestion is also true--that we can not perform an action without having in the mind at the time the appropriate thought, or image, or memory to suggest the action. This dependence of action upon the thought which the mind has at the time is conclusively shown in certain patients having partial paralysis. These patients find that when the eyes are bandaged they can not use their limbs, and it is simply because they can not realize without seeing the limb how it would feel to move it; but open the eyes and let them see the limb--then they move it freely. A patient can not speak when the cortex of the brain is injured in the particular spot which is used in remembering how the words feel or sound when articulated. Many such cases lead to the general position that for each of our intentional actions we must have some way of thinking about the action, of remembering how it feels, looks, etc.; we must have something in mind equivalent to the experience of the movement. This is called the principle of Kinaesthetic Equivalents, an expression which loses its formidable sound when we remember that "kinaesthetic" means having the feeling of movement; so the principle expresses the truth that we must in every case have some thought or mental picture in mind which is equivalent to the feeling of the movement we desire to make; if not, we can not succeed in making it.

What we mean by the "freedom" of the will is not ability to do anything without thinking, but ability to think all the alternatives together and to act on this larger thought. Free action is the fullest expression of thought and of the Self which thinks it.

It is interesting to observe the child getting his Equivalents day by day. He can not perform a new movement simply by wishing to do so; he has no Equivalents in his mind to proceed upon. But as he learns the action, gradually striking the proper movements one by one--oftenest by imitation, as we will see later on--he stores the necessary Equivalents up in his memory, and afterward only needs to think how the movements feel or look, or how words sound, to be able to make the movements or speak the words forthwith.

III. Introspection finds another great class of conditions in experience, again on the receptive side--conditions which convert the mind from the mere theatre of indifferent changes into the vitally interested, warmly intimate thing which our mental life is to each of us. This is the sphere of Feeling. We may see without more ado that while we are receiving sensations and thoughts and suggestions, and acting upon them in the variety of ways already pointed out, we ourselves are not indifferent spectators of this play, this come-and-go of processes. We are directly implicated; indeed, the very sense of a self, an ego, a me-and-mine, in each consciousness, arises from the fact that all this come-and-go is a personal growth. The mind is not a mere machine doing what the laws of its action prescribe. We find that nothing happens which does not affect the mind itself for better or for worse, for richer or for poorer, for pleasure or for pain; and there spring up a series of attitudes of the mind itself, according as it is experiencing or expecting to experience what to it is good or bad. This is, then, the great meaning of Feeling; it is the sense in the mind that it is itself in some way influenced for good or for ill by what goes on within it. It stands midway between thought and action. We feel with reference to what we think, and we act because we feel. All action is guided by feeling.

Feeling shows two well-marked characters: first, the Excitement of taking a positive attitude; and, second, the Pleasure or Pain that goes with it.

Here, again, it may suffice to distinguish the stages which arise as we go from the higher to the lower, from the life of Sensation and Perception up to that of Thought. This was our method in both of the other phases of the mental life--Knowledge and Action. Doing this, therefore, in the case of Feeling also, we find different terms applied to the different phases of feeling. In the lowest sort of mental life, as we may suppose the helpless newborn child to have it, and as we also think it exists in certain low forms of animal life, feeling is not much more than Pleasures and Pains depending largely upon the physical conditions under which life proceeds. It is likely that there are both Pleasures and Pains which are actually sensations with special nerve apparatus of their own; and there are also states of the Comfortable and the Uncomfortable, or of pleasant and unpleasant feeling, due to the way the mind is immediately affected. These are conditions of Excitement added to the Sensations of Pleasure and Pain.

Coming up to the life of Memory and Imagination, we find many great classes of Emotions testifying to the attitudes which the mind takes toward its experiences. They are remarkably rich and varied, these emotions. Hope gives place to its opposite despair, joy to sorrow, and regret succeeds expectation. No one can enumerate the actual phases of the emotional life. The differences which are most pronounced--as between hope and fear, joy and sorrow, anger and love--have special names, and their stimulating causes are so constant that they have also certain fixed ways of showing themselves in the body, the so-called emotional Expressions. It is by these that we see and sympathize with the emotional states of other persons. The most that we have room here to say is that there is a constant ebb and flow, and that we rarely attain a state of relative freedom from the influence of emotion.

The fixed bodily Expressions of emotion are largely hereditary and common to man and the animals. It is highly probable that they first arose as attitudes useful in the animal's environments for defence, flight, seizure, embrace, etc., and have descended to man as survivals, so becoming indications of states of the mind.

The final and highest manifestation of the life of feeling is what we call Sentiment. Sentiment is aroused in response to certain so-called ideal states of thought. The trend of mental growth toward constantly greater adequacy in its knowledge leads it to anticipate conditions when its attainments will be made complete. There are certain sorts of reality whose completeness, thus imagined, arouses in us emotional states of the greatest power and value. The thought of God gives rise to the Religious sentiment, that of the good to the Ethical or Moral sentiment, that of the beautiful to the Esthetic sentiment. These sentiments represent the most refined and noble fruitage of the life of feeling, as the thoughts which they accompany refer to the most elevated and ideal objects. And it is equally true that the conduct which is performed under the inspiration of Sentiment is the noblest and most useful in which man can engage.

CHAPTER III.

THE MIND OF THE ANIMAL--COMPARATIVE PSYCHOLOGY.

It has already been pointed out that the animal has a very important share of the endowment which we call mind. Only recently has he been getting his due. He was formerly looked upon, under the teachings of a dualistic philosophy and of a jealous humanity, as a soulless machine, a mere automaton which was moved by the starting of certain springs to run on until the machine ran down. There are two reasons that this view has been given up, each possibly important enough to have accomplished the revolution and to have given rise to Animal Psychology.

First, there is the rise of the evolution theory, which teaches that there is no absolute break between man and the higher animals in the matter of mental endowment, and that what difference there is must itself be the result of the laws of mental growth; and the second reason is that the more adequate the science of the human mind has become the more evident has it also become that man himself is more of a machine than had been supposed. Man grows by certain laws; his progress is conditioned by the environment, both physical and social, in which he lives; his mind is a part of the natural system of things. So with the animal. The animal fulfils, as far as he can, the same sort of function; he has his environment, both physical and social; he works under the same laws of growth which man also obeys; his mind exhibits substantially the same phenomena which the human mind exhibits in its early stages in the child. All this means that the animal has as good right to recognition, as a mind-bearing creature, so to speak, as the child; and if we exclude him we should also exclude the child. Further, this also means--what is more important for the science of psychology--that the development of the mind in its early stages and in certain of its directions of progress is revealed most adequately in the animals.

Animal Instinct.--Turning to the animals, the first thing to strike us is the remarkable series of so-called animal Instincts. Everybody knows what animal instincts are like; it is only necessary to go to a zo鰈ogical garden to see them in operation on a large scale. Take the house cat and follow her through the life of a single day, observing her actions. She washes her face and makes her toilet in the morning by instinct. She has her peculiar instinctive ways of catching the mouse for breakfast. She whets her appetite by holding back her meal possibly for an hour, in the meantime playing most cruelly with the pitiful mouse, letting it run and catching it again, and doing this over and over. If she has children she attends to their training in the details of cat etiquette and custom with the utmost care, all by instinct; and the kittens instinctively respond to her attentions. She conducts herself during the day with remarkable cleanliness of life, making arrangements which civilized man follows with admiration. She shows just the right abhorrence of water for a creature that is not able to swim. She knows just what enemies to fly from and when to turn and fight, using with inborn dexterity her formidable claws. She prefers nocturnal excursions and sociabilities, having eyes which make it safe to be venturesome in the dark. She has certain vocal expressions of her emotions, which man in vain attempts to eradicate with all the agencies of domestication. She has special arts to attract her mate, and he in turn is able to charm her with songs which charm nobody else. And so on, almost ad infinitum.

Observe the dog, the birds of different species, the monkeys, the hares, and you find wonderful differences of habit, each adapting the animal differently, but with equal effectiveness, to the life which he in particular is called upon to lead. The ants and bees are notoriously expert in the matter of instinct. They have colonies in which some of the latest principles of social organization seem to find analogues: slavery, sexual regulations, division of labour, centralization of resources, government distribution of food, capital punishment, etc.

All this--not to stop upon details which the books on animal life give in great abundance--has furnished grounds for speculation for centuries, and it is only in the last generation that the outlines of a theory of instinct have been filled in with substantial knowledge. A rapid sketch of this theory may be drawn in the following pages.

1. In instinct in general there is a basis of inherited nervous tendency toward the performance of just the sort of action which the instinct exhibits. This nervous tendency shows itself independently of learning by the individual in a

great many cases, as in the instinct of sucking by young animals, pecking for food by young fowls, the migrating actions of adult mammals and birds, the courting movements of many varieties of animal species. In all this we have what is called the "perfect" instinct. To be perfect, an instinct must be carried out successfully by the animal when his organism is ready, without any instruction, any model to imitate, any experience to go upon. The "perfect" instincts are entirely congenital or inborn; the nervous apparatus only needs to reach the proper stage of maturity or growth, and forthwith the instinctive action is performed as soon as the external conditions of life are such as to make its performance appropriate and useful.

2. On the other hand, many instincts--indeed, probably the greater number--are not perfect, but "imperfect." Imperfect instincts are those which do not fully equip the animal with the function in question, but only take him part way to the goal. He has a spontaneous tendency to do certain things, such as building a nest, singing, etc.; but he is not able to do these things adequately or perfectly if left to himself from birth. This sort of endowment with imperfect instincts has been the field of some of the most interesting research in animal psychology, and has led to a new view of the relation of instinct to intelligence.

3. It has been found that young animals, birds, etc., depend upon the example and instruction of adults for the first performance of many actions that seem to be instinctive. This dependence may exist even in cases in which there is yet a congenital tendency to perform the action. Many birds, for example, have a general instinct to build a nest; but in many cases, if put in artificial circumstances, they build imperfect nests. Birds also have an instinct to make vocal calls; but if kept from birth out of hearing of the peculiar notes of their species, they come to make cries of a different sort, or learn to make the notes of some other species with which they are thrown.

4. The principal agency for the learning of the animals, and for the supplementing of their instincts, is Imitation. The sight of certain movements on the part of the adult animals, or the hearing of their cries, calls, notes, etc., leads the young to fall into an imitation of these movements or vocal performances. The endowment which such a young animal has in the direction of making movements and cries similar to those of his species aids him, of course, in imitating these in preference to others. So the endowment

and the tendency to imitate directly aid each other in all such functions, and hurry the little creature on in his acquisition of the habits of his species. We find young animals clinging even in their imitations pretty closely to their own proper fathers and mothers, who are thus enabled to bring them up comme il faut.

5. There is every reason to think, moreover, that the tendency to imitate is itself instinctive. Young animals, notably the monkey and the child, fall spontaneously to imitating when they reach a certain age. Imitation shows itself to be instinctive in the case of the mocking bird, the parrot, etc. Furthermore, the mechanism of this function of imitation is now very well known. The principle of psychology recognised above under the phrase Kinaesthetic Equivalents, teaches us that the idea of a movement, coming into the mind through sight or some other sense, stirs up the proper apparatus to bring about the same movement in the observer. This we see in the common tendency of an audience to repeat the gestures of a speaker, and in many similar cases. When this principle is extended to include all sorts of experiences besides those of movement, we have what is generally called Imitation. Moreover, every time that by action the child imitates, he perceives his own imitation, and this again acts as a "copy" or model for another repetition of the act, and so on. This method of keeping himself going gives the young animal or child constant practice, and renders him more and more efficient in the acts necessary to his life.

6. It is evident what great profit accrues from this arrangement whereby a general instinct like imitation takes the place of a number of special instincts, or supplements them. It gives a measure of plasticity to the creature. He can now respond suitably to changes in the environment in which he lives. The special instincts, on the contrary, are for the most part so fixed that the animal must act just as they require him to in this or that circumstance; but as soon as his instinct takes on the form of imitation, the resulting action tends to conform itself to the model actions of the other creatures which set "copies" before him.

These more or less new results due to recent research in the province of Instinct have had direct bearing upon theories of the origin of instinct and of its place in animal life.

Theories of Instinct.--Apart from the older view which saw in animal instinct simply a matter of original created endowment, whereby each animal was made once for all "after his kind," and according to which there is no further reason that the instincts are what they are than that they were made so; apart from this "special creation" view, two different ideas have had currency, both based upon the theory of evolution. Each of these views assumes that the instincts have been developed from more simple animal actions by a gradual process; but they differ as to the elements originally entering into the actions which afterward became instinctive.

1. First, there is what is called the Reflex Theory. This holds that instincts are reflex actions, like the closing of the eye when an object threatens to enter it, only much more complex. They are due to the compounding and adding together of simple reflexes, in greater and greater number, and with increasing efficiency. This theory attempts to account for instinct entirely in terms of nervous action. It goes with that view of evolution which holds that the nervous system has had its growth from generation to generation by the continued reflex adjustments of the organism to its environment, whereby more and more delicate adaptations to the external world were secured. In this way, say the advocates of this theory, we may account for the fact that the animal has no adequate knowledge of what he is doing when he performs an act instinctively; he has no end or aim in his mind; he simply feels his nervous system doing what it is fitted to do by its organic adaptations to the stimulations of air, and earth, and sea, whatever these may be.

But it may be asked: Why do succeeding generations improve each on its parents, so that there is a gradual tendency to perfect the instinct?

The answer to this question brings up another great law of biology--the principle of Variations. This principle states the common fact that in every case of a family of offspring the individual young vary slightly in all directions from their parents. Admitting this, we will find in each group of families some young individuals which are better than their parents; these will have the advantage over others and will be the ones to grow up and have the children of the next generation again, and so on. So by constant Variation and Natural Selection--that is, the "Survival of the Fittest" in competition with the rest-- there will be constant improvement in the Instinct.

2. The other theory, the rival one, holds that there are some instincts which show so plainly the marks of Reason that some degree of intelligent adjustment to the environment must be allowed to the animal in the acquiring of these functions. For example, we are told that some of the muscular movements involved in the instincts--such, for example, as the bird's nest-building--are so complex and so finely adjusted to an end, that it is straining belief to suppose that they could have arisen gradually by reflex adaptation alone. There is also a further difficulty with the reflex theory which has seemed insurmountable to many of the ablest psychologists of animal life; the difficulty, namely, that many of the instincts require the action of a great many muscles at the same time, so acting in "correlation" with or support of one another that it is impossible to suppose that the instinct has been acquired gradually. For in the very nature of these cases we can not suppose the instinct to have ever been imperfect, seeing that the partial instinct which would have preceded the perfect performance for some generations would have been not only of no use to the creature, but in many cases positively injurious. For instance, what use to an animal to be able partly to make the movements of swimming, or to the birds to build an inadequate nest? Such instincts would not be usable at all. So we are told by the second theory that the animals must have had intelligence to do these things when they first acquired them. Yet, as is everywhere admitted, after the instinct has been acquired by the species it is then carried out without knowledge and intelligent design, being handed down from generation to generation by heredity.

This seems reasonable, for we do find that actions which were at first intelligent may be performed so frequently that we come to do them without thinking of them; to do them from habit. So the animals, we are told, have come to do theirs reflexly, although at first they required intelligence. From this point of view--that although intelligence was at first required, yet the actions have become instinctive and lacking in intelligent direction in later generations--this is called the theory of Lapsed Intelligence.

This theory has much to commend it. It certainly meets the objection to the reflex theory which was stated just above--the objection that some of the instincts could not have arisen by gradual reflex adaptations. It also accounts for the extremely intelligent appearance which many instincts have.

But this view in turn is liable to a criticism which has grown in force with the progress of biological knowledge in recent years. This criticism is based on the fact that the theory of lapsed intelligence demands that the actions which the animals of one generation have acquired by their intelligence should be handed down through heredity to the next generation, and so on. It is evident that unless this be true it does no good to the species for one generation to do things intelligently, seeing that if the effects on the nervous system are not transmitted to their children, then the next and later generations will have to start exactly where their fathers did, and the actions in question will never become ingrained in the nervous system at all.

Now, the force of this criticism is overwhelming to those who believe--as the great majority of biologists now do[1]--that none of the modifications or so-called "characters" acquired by the parents, none of the effects of use or disuse of their limbs, none of the tendencies or habits of action, in short, none of the changes wrought in body or mind of the parents during their lifetime, are inherited by their children. The only sorts of modification which show themselves in subsequent generations are the deep-seated effects of disease, poison, starvation, and other causes which concern the system as a whole, but which show no tendency to reproduce by heredity any of the special actions or functions which the fathers and mothers may have learned and practised. If this difficulty could be met, the theory that intelligence has been at work in the origination of the complex instincts would be altogether the preferable one of the two; but if not, then the "lapsed intelligence" view must be thrown overboard.

[Footnote 1: The matter is still under discussion, however, and I do not mean in any way to deny the authority of those who still accept the "inheritance of acquired characters."]

Recent discussion of evolution has brought out a point of view under the name of Organic Selection which has a very fruitful application to this controversy over the origin of instincts. This point of view is one which in a measure reconciles the two theories. It claims that it is possible for the intelligent adaptations, or any sort of "accommodations," made by the individuals of one generation, to set the direction of subsequent evolution, even though there be no direct inheritance of acquired characters from father to son. It proceeds in the case of instinct somewhat thus:

Suppose we say, with the first theory given above, that the organism has certain reflexes which show some degree of adaptation to the environment; then suppose we admit the point, urged by the advocates of the lapsed intelligence theory, that the gradual improvement of these reflexes by variations in the endowment of successive generations would not suffice for the origin of instinct, seeing that partial instincts would not be useful; and, further, suppose we agree that many of the complex instincts really involved intelligent adaptation in their acquisition. These points carefully understood, then one new and further principle will enable us to complete a theory which will avoid the objections to both the others. This principle is nothing else than what we have seen already--namely, that the intelligence supplements the partial instincts in each generation and makes them useful in the respects in which they are inadequate, and so keeps the young alive in successive generations as long as the instinct is imperfect. This gives the species time gradually to supplement its instinctive endowment, in the course of many generations each of which uses its intelligence in the same way: time to accumulate, by the occurrence of variations among the offspring, the changes in the nervous system which the perfect instinct requires. Thus as time goes on the dependence of each generation upon the aid of intelligence is less and less, until the nervous system becomes capable of performing the function quite alone. The result then will be the same as if the acquisitions made by each generation had been inherited, while in reality they have not. All that this theory requires in addition to what is admitted by both the historical views is that the species be kept alive long enough by the aid of its intelligence, which supplements imperfect instincts, to give it time to produce sufficient variations in the right direction. The instinct then achieves its independence, and intelligent supervision of it is no longer necessary (see Fig. 1).

[Illustration: FIG. 1,--Origin of instinct by Organic Selection: A n, perfect instinct. 1, 2 ... n, successive generations. Solid lines, nervous equipment in the direction of the instinct. Dotted lines, intelligence supplementing the nervous equipment. The intelligence is relied upon to keep the species alive until by congenital variations the nervous equipment becomes "perfect."]

This theory is directly confirmed by the facts, already spoken of, which show that many instincts are imperfect, but are pieced out and made effective by the intelligent imitations and acquisitions of the young creatures. The little chick, for example, does not know the value of water when he sees it, as essential as water is to his life; but he depends upon imitation of his mother's drinking, or upon the mere accident of wetting his bill, to stimulate his partial instinct of drinking in the peculiar fashion characteristic of fowls, by throwing back the head. So in other functions which are peculiar to a species and upon which their very lives depend, we find the delicate adjustment between intelligent adaptation by conscious action and the partially formed instincts which the creatures possess.

In the theory of Organic Selection, therefore, we seem to have a positive solution of the question of the origin of instinct. It is capable of a similar application in other cases where evolution has taken certain definite directions, seemingly guided by intelligence. It shows us that mind has had a positive place in the evolution of organic nature.

* * * * *

Animal Intelligence.--Coming to consider what further equipment the animals have, we light upon the fact just spoken of when we found it necessary to appeal in some measure to the animal's Intelligence to supplement his instincts. What is meant by Intelligence?

This word may be used in the broad sense of denoting all use of consciousness, or mind, considered as a thing in some way additional to the reflexes of the nervous system. In the life of the animal, as in that of man, wherever we find the individual doing anything with reference to a mental picture, using knowledge or experience in any form, then he is said to be acting intelligently.

The simplest form of intelligent action in the animal world and that from which most of the higher forms have arisen is illustrated in the following example: a chick will peck at a strange worm, and, finding it unpalatable, will then in the future refuse to peck at worms of that sort. This refusal to do a second time what has once had a disagreeable result is intelligent. We now say that the chick "knows" that the worm is not good to eat. The instinctive action of pecking at all worms is replaced by a refusal to peck at certain worms. Again, taking the reverse case, we find that the chick which did not respond to the sight of drinking water instinctively, but had to see the mother drink first, acted intelligently, or through a state of consciousness, when it imitated the old hen, and afterward drank of its own accord. It now "knows" that water is the thing to drink.

The further question which comes upon us here concerns the animal's acquisition of the action appropriate to carry out his knowledge. How does he learn the muscular combinations which supplement or replace the earlier instinctive ways of acting?

This question appears very clearly when we ask about the child's acquisition of new acts of skill. We find him constantly learning, modifying his habits, refining his ways of doing things, becoming possessed of quite new and complex functions, such as speech, handwriting, etc. All these are intelligent activities; they are learned very gradually and with much effort and pains. It is one of the most important and interesting questions of all psychology to ask how he manages to bring the nervous and muscular systems under greater and greater control by his mind. How can he modify and gradually improve his "reactions"--as we call his responses to the things and situations about him--so as to act more and more intelligently?

The answer seems to be that he proceeds by what has been called Experimenting. He does not simply do things because he has intelligence,--simply that is, because he sees how to do them without first learning how; that is the older and probably quite erroneous view of intelligence. The mind can not move the body simply by its fiat. No man can do that. Man, like the little animal, has to try things and keep on trying things, in order to find out the way they work and what their possibilities are. And each animal, man, beast, or bird has to do it for himself. Apart from the instinctive actions which the child does without knowing their value at all, and apart from the equally instinctive imitative way of doing them without aiming at learning more by the imitations, he proceeds in all cases to make experiments. Generally his experiments work through acts of imitation. He imitates what he sees some other creature do; or he imitates his own instinctive actions by setting up before him in his mind the memories of the earlier performance; or, yet again, after he has struck a fortunate combination, he repeats that imitatively. Thus, by the principle already spoken of, he stores up a great mass of Kinaesthetic Equivalents, which linger in memory, and enable him to act appropriately when the proper circumstances come in his way. He also gets what we have called Associations established between the acts and the pleasure or pain which they give, and so avoids the painful and repeats the pleasurable ones.

The most fruitful field of this sort of imitative learning is in connection with the "try-try-again" struggles of the young, especially children. This is called Persistent Imitation. The child sees before him some action to imitate--some complex act of manipulation with the hand, let us say. He tries to perform it in an experimental way, using the muscles of the hand and arm. With this he strains himself all over, twisting his tongue, bending his body, and grimacing from head to foot, so to speak. Thus he gets a certain way toward the correct result, but very crudely and inexactly. Then he tries again, proceeding now on the knowledge which the first effort gave him; and his trial is less uncouth because he now suppresses some of the hindering grimacing movements and retains the ones which he sees to be most nearly correct. Again he tries, and again, persistently but gradually reducing the blundering movements to the pattern of the copy, and so learning to perform the act of skill.

The massive and diffused movements which he makes by wriggling and fussing are also of direct use to him. They increase remarkably the chances that among them all there will be some movements which will hit the mark, and so contribute to his stock of correct Equivalents. Dogs and monkeys learn to unlock doors, let down fence rails, and perform relatively complex actions by experimenting; persistently with many varied movements until the successful ones are finally struck.

This is the type of all those acts of experimenting by which new complex movements are acquired. In children it proceeds largely without interference from others; the child persists of himself. He has greater ability than the animals to see the meaning of the completed act and to really desire to acquire it. With the animals the acquisitions do not extend very far, on account of their limitation in intelligent endowment; but in the training of the domestic animals and in the education of show-animals the trainer aids them and urges them on by making use of the associations of pleasure and pain spoken of above. He supplements the animal's feelings of pain and pleasure with the whip and with rewards of food, etc., so that each step of the animal's success or failure has acute associations with pain or pleasure. Thus the animal gradually gets a number of associations formed, avoids the actions with which pain is associated, repeats those which call up memories of pleasure all the way through an extended performance in regular steps; and in the result the performance so closely counterfeits the operations of high intelligence--such as counting, drawing cards, etc.--that the audience is excited to admiration.

This first glimpse of the animal's limitations when compared with man may suggest the general question, how far the brutes go in their intelligent endowment. The proper treatment of this much-debated point requires certain further explanations.

In the child we find a tendency to act in certain ways toward all objects, events, etc., which are in any respect alike. After learning to use the hands, for example, for a certain act, the same hand movements are afterward used for other similar acts which the child finds it well to perform. He thus tends, as psychologists say, to "generalize," that is, to take up certain general attitudes which will answer for a great many details of experience. On the side of the reception of his items of knowledge this was called Assimilation, as will be remembered. This saves him enormous trouble and risk; for as soon as an object or situation presents itself before him with certain general aspects, he can at once take up the attitude appropriate to these general aspects without waiting to learn the particular features of the new. The ability to do this shows itself in two rather different ways which seem respectively to characterize man on the one hand and the lower animals on the other.

With the animals this tendency to generalize, to treat objects in classes rather than as individuals, takes the form of a sort of composition or direct union of brain pathways. Different experiences are had, and then because they are alike they tend to issue in the same channels of action. The animal is tied down strictly to his experience; he does not anticipate to any extent what is going to happen. He does not use one experience as a symbol and apply it beforehand to other things and events. He is in a sense passive; stimulations rain down upon him, and force him into certain attitudes and ways of action. As far as his knowledge is "general" it is called a Recept. A dog has a Recept of the whip; so far as whips are not too different from one another, the dog will act in the same way toward all of them. In man, on the other hand, the development of mind has gone a decided step further. The child very quickly begins to use symbols, words being the symbols of first importance to him. He does not have, like the brute, to wait for successive experiences of like objects to impress themselves upon him; but he goes out toward the new, expecting it to be like the old, and so acting as to anticipate it. He thus falls naturally into general ways of acting which it is the function of experience to refine and distinguish. He seems to have more of the higher sort of what was called above Apperception, as opposed to the more concrete and accidental Associations of Ideas. He gets Concepts, as opposed to the Recepts of the animals. With this goes the development of speech, which some psychologists consider the source of all the man's superiority over the animals. Words become symbols of a highly abstract sort for certain classes of experiences; and, moreover, through speech a means of social communication is afforded by which the development of the individual is enormously advanced.

It is probable, in fact, that this difference--that between the Generalization which uses symbols, and mere Association--is the root of all the differences that follow later on, and give man the magnificent advantage over the animals which he has. From it is developed the faculty of thinking, reasoning, etc., in which man stands practically alone. On the brain side, it requires special developments both through the preparation of certain brain centres given over to the speech function, and also through the greater organization of the gray matter of the cerebral cortex, to which we revert again in a later chapter. Indeed, looked at from the side of the development of the brain, we see that there is no break between man and the animals in the laws of organization, but that the difference is one of evolution.

Later on in the life of the child we find another contrast connected with the difference of social life and organization as between the animals and man. The animals probably do not have a highly organized sense of Self as man does; and the reason doubtless is that such a Self-consciousness is the outcome of life and experience in the very complex social relations in which the human child is brought up, and which he alone is fitted by his inherited gifts to sustain.

The Play of Animals.--Another of the most interesting questions of animal life is that which concerns their plays. Most animals are given to play. Indeed that they indulge in a remarkable variety of sports is well known even to the novice in the study of their habits. Beginning when very young, they gambol, tussle, leap, and run together, chase one another, play with inanimate objects, as the kitten with the ball, join in the games of children and adults, as the dog which plays hide and seek with his little master, and all with a knowingness and zest which makes them the best of companions. The volumes devoted to the subject give full accounts of these plays of animals, and we need not repeat them; the psychologist is interested, however, mainly in the general function of play in the life of the individual animal and child, and in the psychological states and motives which it reveals. Play, whether in animals or in man, shows certain general characteristics which we may briefly consider.

1. The plays of animals are very largely instinctive, being indulged in for the most part without instruction. The kitten leaps impulsively to the game. Little dogs romp untaught, and fall, as do other animals also, when they are strong enough, into all the playful attitudes which mark their kind. This is seen strikingly among adult animals in what are called the courtship plays. The birds, for example, indulge in elaborate and beautiful evolutions of a playful sort at the mating season.

2. It follows from their instinctive character that animal plays are peculiar to the species which perform them. We find series of sports peculiar to dogs, others to cats, and so on through all the species of the zoological garden, whether the creatures be wild or tame. Each shows its species as clearly by its sportive habits as by its shape, cry, or any other of what are called its "specific" habits. This is important not only to the zoologist, as indicating differences of evolution and scale of attainment, environment, etc., but also to the psychologist, as indicating differences of what we may call animal temperament. Animals show not only the individual differences which human beings do, one liking this game and another that, one being leader in the sport and another the follower, but also the greater differences which characterize races. The Spaniards love the bull fight; other nations consider it repulsive, and take their fun in less brutal forms, although, perchance, they tolerate Rugby football! So the animals vary in their tastes, some playing incessantly at fighting, and so zealously as to injure one another, while others like the milder romp, and the game with flying leaves, rolling stones, or the incoming waves on the shore.

3. Psychologically, the most interesting characteristic of animal, as of human, play is what is called the "make-believe" state of mind which enters into it. If we consider our own sports we find that, in the midst of the game, we are in a condition of divided consciousness. We indulge in the scheme of play, whatever it be, as if it were a real situation, at the same time preserving our sense that it is not real. That is, we distinguish through it all the actual realities, but make the convention with our companions that for the time we will act together as if the playful situation were real. With it there is a sense that it is a matter of voluntary indulgence that can stop at anytime; that the whole temporary illusion to which we submit is strictly our own doing, a job which we have "put up" on ourselves. That is what is meant by make-believe.

Now it is clear that the animals have this sense of make-believe in their games both with other animals and with man. The dog plays at biting the hand of his master, and actually takes the member between his teeth and mumbles it; but all the while he stops short of painful pressure, and goes through a series of characteristic attitudes which show that he distinguishes very clearly between this play biting and the real. If perchance the master shows signs of being hurt, the dog falls into attitudes of sorrow, and apologizes fulsomely. So also when the animals play together, a vigorous squeal from a companion who is "under" generally brings him his release.

The principal interest of this make-believe consciousness is that it is considered by many to be an essential ingredient of 苊 thetic feeling. A work of art is said to have its effect through its tendency to arouse in us a make-believe acceptance of the scene or motive presented, while it nevertheless remains contrasted with the realities of our lives. If this be true, the interesting question arises how far the animals also have the germs of 苊 thetic feeling in their make-believe situations. Does the female pea-fowl consider the male bird, with all his display of colour and movement, a beautiful object? And does the animal companion say: How beautiful! when his friend in the sport makes a fine feint, and comes up serene with the knowing look, which the human on-looker can not fail to understand?

In some cases, at any rate, we should have to reply to this question affirmatively, if we considered make-believe the essential thing in aesthetic enjoyment.

Theories of Animal Play.--The question of the meaning and value of play to the animals has had very enlightening discussion of late. There are two principal theories now advocated.

I. The older theory considered play simply the discharge of surplus nerve force in the animal's organism. He was supposed to play when he felt fresh and vigorous. The horse is "skittish" and playful in the morning, not so much so at night. The dogs lie down and rest when they are tired, having used up their surplus energies. This is called the Surplus-Energy Theory of play.

The difficulty with this theory is that it is not adequate to explain any of the characteristics of play which have been given above. Why should play be instinctive in its forms, showing certain complex and ingrained channels of expression, if it were merely the discharge of surplus force? We are more lively in the morning, but that does not explain our liking and indulging in certain sorts of complex games at all hours. Moreover, animals and children will continue to play when greatly fatigued. A dog, for example, which seems absolutely "used up," can not resist the renewed solicitations of his friends to continue the chase. Furthermore, why is it that plays are characteristic of species, different kinds of animals having plays quite peculiar to themselves? It is difficult to see how this could have come about unless there had been some deeper-going reason in accordance with which each species has learned the particular forms of sport in which it indulges.

The advocates of this theory attempt to meet these objections by saying that the imitative instinct accounts for the particular directions in which the discharges of energy occur. A kitten's plays are like those of the cat tribe because the kitten is accustomed to imitate cats; when it falls to playing it is with cats, and so it sheds its superfluous energies in the customary imitative channels. In this way it grows to learn the games of its own species. There is a good deal in this point; most games are imitative in so far as they are learned at all. But it does not save the theory; for many animal plays are not learned by the individual at all, as we have seen above; on the contrary, they are instinctive. In these cases the animal does not wait to learn the games of his tribe by imitation, but starts-right-in on his own account. Besides this there are many forms of animal play which are not imitative at all. In these the animals co-operate, but do not take the same parts. The young perform actions in the game which the mother does not.

All this goes to support another and most serious objection to this theory--in the mind of all those who believe in the doctrine of evolution. The Surplus-Energy Theory considers the play-impulse, which is one of the most widespread characters of animal life, as merely an accidental thing or by-product--a mere using-up of surplus energies. It is not in any way important to the animals. This makes it impossible to say that play has come to be the very complex thing that it really is by the laws of evolution; for survival by natural selection always supposes that the attribute or character which survives is important enough to keep the animal alive in the struggle for existence; otherwise it would not be continued for successive generations, and gradually perfected on account of its utility.

On the whole, therefore, we find the Surplus-Energy Theory of play quite inadequate.

II. Another theory therefore becomes necessary if we are to meet these difficulties. Such a theory has recently been developed. It holds that the plays of the animals are of the greatest utility to them in this way: they exercise the young animals in the very activities--though in a playful way--in which they must seriously engage later on in life. A survey of the plays of animals with a view to comparing them in each case with the adult activities of the same species, confirms this theory in a remarkably large number of cases. It shows the young anticipating, in their play, the struggles, enjoyments, co-operations, defeats, emergencies, etc., of their after lives, and by learning to cope with all these situations, so preparing themselves for the serious onset of adult responsibilities. On this theory each play becomes a beautiful case of adaptation to nature. The kitten plays with the ball as the old cat handles the mouse; the little dogs wrestle together, and so learn to fight with teeth and claws; the deer run from one another, and so test their speed and learn to escape their enemies. If we watch young animals at play we see that not a muscle or nerve escapes this preliminary training and exercise; and the instinctive tendencies which control the play direct the activities into just the performances which the animal's later life-habits are going on to require.

On this view play becomes of the utmost utility. It is not a by-product, but an essential part of the animal's equipment. Just as the infancy period has been lengthened in the higher animals in order to give the young time to learn all that they require to meet the harsh conditions of life, so during this infancy period they have in the play-instinct a means of the first importance for making good use of their time. It is beautiful to see the adults playing with their young, adapting their strength to the little ones, repeating the same exercises without ceasing, drilling them with infinite pains to greater hardihood, endurance, and skill.

On this theory it is also easy to see why it is that the plays are different for the different species. The actual life conditions are different, and the habits of the species are correspondingly different. So it is only another argument for the truth of this theory that we find just those games natural to the young which train them in the habits natural to the old.

This view is now being very generally adopted. Many fine illustrations might be cited. A simple case may be seen in so small a thing as the habit of leaping in play; the difference, for example, between the mountain goat and the common fawn. The former, when playing on level ground makes a very ludicrous exhibition by jumping in little up-and-down leaps by which he makes no progress. In contrast with this the fawn, whose adult life is normally in the plains, takes a long graceful spring. The difference becomes clear from the point of view of this theory, when we remember that the goat is to live among the rocks, where the only useful jump is just the up-and-down sort which the little fellow is now practising; while the deer, in his life upon the plains, will always need the running jump.

Finally, on this theory, play becomes a thing for evolution to cultivate for its utility in the progress of animal life, and for that reason we may suppose it has been perfected in the remarkable variety and beauty of form which it shows.

On the psychological side, we find a corresponding state of things. The mind in the young animal or child gets the main education of early life through its play situations. Games have an extraordinary pedagogical influence. The more so because they are the natural and instinctive way of getting an education in practical things. This again is of supreme utility to the individuals.

Both for body and mind we find that play illustrates the principle of Organic Selection explained above. It makes the young animal flexible, plastic, and adaptable; it supplements all his other instincts and imperfect functions; it gives him a new chance to live, and so determines the course of evolution in the direction which the playful animal represents. The quasi-social and gregarious habits of animals probably owe much of their strength to the play-impulse, both through the training of individual animals and through the fixing of these tendencies as instincts in various animal species in the way just mentioned.

In another place below I analyze a child's game and draw some inferences from it. Here it may suffice to say that in their games the young animals acquire the flexibility of mind and muscle upon which much of the social co-operation, as well as the individual effectiveness, of their later life depends. With children, it is not the only agency, of course, though its importance is not less. We have to carry the children further by other means; but the other means should never interfere with this natural schooling. They should aim the rather by supplementing it wisely to direct its operation and to extend its sphere.

CHAPTER IV.

THE MIND OF THE CHILD--CHILD PSYCHOLOGY.

One of the most interesting chapters of modern psychology is that which deals with the child. This is also one of the topics of general concern, since our common humanity reacts with greater geniality upon the little ones, in whom we instinctively see innocence and simplicity. The popular interest in children has been, however--as uncharitable as it may seem to say it--of very little service to the scientific investigation of childhood. Even to-day, when a greater body of valuable results are being secured, the main danger to the proper study of the child's mind comes from the over-enthusiasm and uninstructed assurance of some of its friends. Especially is this the case in America, where "child study" has become a fad to be pursued by parents and teachers who know little about the principles of scientific method, and where influential educators have enlisted so-called "observers" in taking indiscriminate notes on the doings of children with no definite problem in view, and with no criticism of their procedure. It is in place, therefore, to say clearly, at the outset, that this chapter does not mean to stimulate parents or unpsychological readers to report observations; and further to say also that in the mind of the writer the publications made lately of large numbers of replies to "syllabi" are for the most part worthless, because they heap together observations obtained by persons of every degree of competence and incompetence.

On the other hand, the requisites here, as in every other sphere of exact observation, are clear enough. The student of the child's mind should have a thorough knowledge of the principles of general psychology, in order to know what is characteristic of the child when he sees it, and what is exceptional; and he should also have enough originality in his ideas and interpretations to catch the valuable in the child's doings, distinguishing it from the commonplace, and to plan situations and even experiments which will give him some control upon those actions of the child which seem to be worth it. The need of these qualities is seen in the history of the problems of the child's growth which have been taken up even by the most competent psychologists. The results show a gradual attainment of control over the problem in hand, each observer criticising the method and results of his predecessor until certain rules of observation and experiment have been evolved which allow of the repetition and repeated observation of the events of the child's life.

As illustrating the sort of problems in which there has been this careful and critical work, I may instance these: the child's reflex movements, the beginnings and growth of sensation, such as colour, the rise of discrimination and preference, the origin of right and left-handedness, the rise, mechanism, and meaning of imitation, the acquisition of speech and handwriting, the growth of the child's sense of personality and of his social consciousness, and the laws of physical growth, as bearing upon mental development. In all these cases, however, there is again a greater and a less exactness. The topics with the reports of results which I am going on to give may be taken, however, as typical, and as showing the direction of complete knowledge rather than as having in any one case approached it.

Before we take up particular questions, however, a word may be allowed upon the general bearings of the study of the child's mind. I do this the more willingly, since it is still true, in spite of the hopeful outlook for positive results, that it is mainly the willingness of psychology to recognise the problems and work at them that makes the topic important at present. To investigate the child by scientific methods is really to bring into psychology a procedure which has revolutionized the natural sciences; and it is destined to revolutionize the moral sciences by making them also in a great measure natural sciences. The new and important question about the mind which is thus recognised is this: How did it grow? What light upon its activity and nature can we get from a positive knowledge of its early stages and processes of growth? This at once introduces other questions: How is the growth of the child related to that of the animals?--how, through heredity and social influences, to the growth of the race and of the family and society in which he is brought up? All this can be comprehended only in the light of the doctrine of evolution, which has rejuvenated the sciences of life; and we are now beginning to see a rejuvenation of the sciences of mind from the same point of view. This is what is meant when we hear it said that psychology is becoming "genetic."

The advantages to be derived from the study of young children from this point of view may be briefly indicated.

1. In the first place, the facts of the infant consciousness are very simple; that is, they are the child's sensations or memories simply, not his own observations of them. In the adult mind the disturbing influence of self-observation is a matter of notorious moment. It is impossible for me to report exactly what I feel, for the observation of it by my attention alters its character. My volition also is a complex thing, involving my personal pride and self-consciousness. But the child's emotion is as spontaneous as a spring. The effects of it in the mental life come out in action, pure and uninfluenced by calculation and duplicity and adult reserve. There is around every one of us adults a web of convention and prejudice of our own making. Not only do we reflect the social formalities of our environment, and thus lose the distinguishing spontaneities of childhood, but each of us builds up his own little world of seclusion and formality with himself. We are subject, as Bacon said, not only to "idols of the forum," but also to "idols of the den."

The child, on the contrary, has not learned his own importance, his pedigree, his beauty, his social place, his religion; he has not observed himself through all these and countless other lenses of time, place, and circumstance. He has not yet turned himself into an idol nor the world into a temple; and we can study him apart from the complex accretions which are the later deposits of his self-consciousness.

2. The study of children is often the only means of testing the truth of our analyses. If we decide that a certain mental state is due to a union of simpler elements, then we may appeal to the proper period of child life to see the union taking place. The range of growth is so enormous from the infant to the adult, and the beginnings of the child's mental life are so low in the scale, in the matter of mental endowment, that there is hardly a question of analysis now under debate in psychology which may not be tested by this method.

At this point it is that child psychology is more valuable than the study of the mind of animals. The latter never become men, while children do. The animals represent in some few respects a branch of the tree of growth in advance of man, while being in many other respects very far behind him. In studying animals we are always haunted by the fear that the analogy from him to man may not hold; that some element essential to the development of the human mind may not be in the animal at all. Even in such a question as the localization of the functions of the brain described later on, where the analogy is one of comparative anatomy and only secondarily of psychology, the monkey presents analogies with man which dogs do not. But in the study of children we may be always sure that a normal child has in him the promise of a normal man.

3. Again, in the study of the child's mind we have the added advantage of a corresponding simplicity on the bodily side; we are able to take account of the physiological processes at a time when they are relatively simple--that is, before the nervous system has grown to maturity. For example, psychology used to hold that we have a "speech faculty," an inborn mental endowment which is incapable of further analysis; but support for the position is wanting when we turn to the brain of the infant. Not only do we fail to find the series of centres now known to be the "speech zone," but even those of them which we do find have not yet taken up this function, either alone or together. In other words, the primary object of each of the various centres involved is not speech, but some other and simpler function; and speech arises by development from a union of these separate functions.

4. In observing young children, a more direct application of experiment is possible. By "experiment" here I mean both experiment on the senses and

also experiment directly on consciousness by suggestion, social influence, etc. In experimenting on adults, great difficulties arise through the fact that reactions--such as performing a voluntary movement when a signal is heard, etc.--are complicated by deliberation, habit, custom, choice, etc. The subject hears a sound, identifies it, and presses a button--if he choose and agree to do so. What goes on in this interval between the advent of the incoming nerve process and the discharge of the outgoing nerve process? Something, at any rate, which represents a brain process of great complexity. Now, anything that fixes or simplifies the brain process, in so far gives greater certainty to the results. For this reason experiments on reflex actions are valuable and decisive where similar experiments on voluntary actions are uncertain and of doubtful value. Now the child's mind is relatively simple, and so offers a field for more fruitful experiment; this is seen in the reactions of the infant to strong stimuli, such as bright colours, etc., as related further on.

With this inadequate review of the advantages of infant psychology, it is well also to point out the dangers of the abuse of it. Such dangers are real. The very simplicity which seems to characterize the life of the child is often extremely misleading, and this because the simplicity in question is sometimes ambiguous. Two actions of the child may appear equally simple; but one may be an adaptive action, learned with great pains and really very complex, while the other may be inadaptive and really simple. Children differ under the law of heredity very remarkably, even in the simplest manifestations of their conscious lives. It is never safe to say without qualification: "This child did, consequently all children must." The most we can usually say in observing single children is: "This child did, consequently another child may."

Speaking more positively, the following remarks may be useful to those who have a mind to observe children:

1. In the first place, we can fix no absolute time in the history of the child at which a certain mental process takes its rise. The observations, now quite extensively recorded, and sometimes quoted as showing that the first year, or the second year, etc., brings such and such developments, tend, on the contrary, to show that such divisions do not hold in any strict sense. Like any other organic growth, the nervous system may develop faster under more favourable conditions, or more slowly under less favourable; and the growth

of the mind is largely dependent upon the growth of the brain. Only in broad outline and within very wide limits can such periods be marked off at all.

2. The possibility of the occurrence of a mental state at a particular time must be distinguished from its necessity. The occurrence of a single clearly observed fact is decisive only against the theory according to which its occurrence under the given conditions may not occur. For example, the very early adaptive movements of the infant in receiving its food can not be due to intelligence and will; but the case is still open as to the question what is the reason of their presence--i.e., how much nervous development is present, how much experience is necessary, etc. It is well to emphasize the fact that one case may be decisive in overthrowing a theory, but the conditions are seldom simple enough to make one case decisive in establishing a theory.

3. It follows, however, from the principle of growth itself that the order of development of the main mental functions is constant, and normally free from great variations; consequently, the most fruitful observations of children are those which show that such an act was present before another. The complexity becomes finally so remarkable that there seems to be no before or after at all in mental things; but if the child's growth shows a stage in which any process is clearly absent, we have at once light upon the laws of growth. For instance: if a single case is conclusively established of a child's drawing an inference before it begins to use words or significant vocal sounds, the one case is as good as a thousand to show that thought may develop in some degree independently of spoken language.

4. While the most direct results are acquired by systematic experiments with a given point in view, still general observations carefully recorded by competent persons, are important for the interpretation which a great many such records may afford in the end. In the multitude of experiences here, as everywhere, there is strength. Such observations should cover everything about the child--his movements, cries, impulses, sleep, dreams, personal preferences, muscular efforts, attempts at expression, games, favourites, etc.--and should be recorded in a regular daybook at the time of occurrence. What is important and what is not, is, as I have said, something to be learned; and it is extremely desirable that any one contemplating such observations should acquaint himself beforehand with the principles of general psychology and physiology, and should seek also the practical advice of a trained

observer.

As yet many of the observations which we have in this field were made by the average mother, who knows less about the human body than she does about the moon or the wild flowers, or by the average father, who sees his child for an hour a day, when the boy is dressed up, and who has never slept in the same room with him--let alone the same bed!--in his life; by people who have never heard the distinction between reflex and voluntary action, or that between nervous adaptation and conscious choice. The difference between the average mother and the good psychologist is this: she has no theories, he has; he has no interests, she has. She may bring up a family of a dozen and not be able to make a single trustworthy observation; he maybe able, from one sound of one yearling, to confirm theories of the neurologist and educator, which are momentous for the future training and welfare of the child.

As for experimenting with children, only the psychologist should undertake it. The connections between the body and the mind are so close in infancy, the mere animal can do so much to ape reason, and the child is so helpless under the leading of instinct, impulse, and external necessity, that the task is excessively difficult--to say nothing of the extreme delicacy and tenderness of the budding tendrils of the mind. But others do experiment! Every time we send a child out of the home to the school, we subject him to experiment of the most serious and alarming kind. He goes into the hands of a teacher who is often not only not wise unto the child's salvation, but who is, perchance, a machine for administering a single experiment to an infinite variety of children. It is perfectly certain that a great many of our children are irretrievably damaged or hindered in their mental and moral development in the school; but we can not be at all sure that they would fare any better if they were taught at home! The children are experimented with so much and so unwisely, in any case, that possibly a little intentional experiment, guided by real insight and psychological information, would do them good.

Methods of experimenting with Children.--In endeavouring to bring such questions as the degree of memory, recognition, association, etc., present in an infant, to a practical test, considerable embarrassment has always been experienced in understanding the child's vocal and other responses. Of course, the only way a child's mind can be studied is through its expressions, facial, lingual, vocal, muscular; and the first question--i.e., What did the infant do? must be followed by a second--i.e., What did his doing that mean? The second question is, as I have said, the harder question, and the one which requires more knowledge and insight. It is evident, on the surface, that the further away we get in the child's life from simple inherited or reflex responses, the more complicated do the processes become, and the greater becomes the difficulty of analyzing them, and arriving at a true picture of the real mental condition which lies back of them.

To illustrate this confusion, I may cite one of the few problems which psychologists have attempted to solve by experiments on children: the determination of the order of rise of the child's perceptions of the different colours. The first series of experiments consisted in showing the child various colours and requiring him to name them, the results being expressed in percentages of correct answers to the whole number. Now this experiment involves no less than four different questions, and the results give absolutely no clew to their separation. It involves:

1. The child's distinguishing different colours displayed simultaneously before it, together with the complete development of the eyes for colour sensation. 2. The child's ability to recognise or identify a colour after having seen it once. 3. An association between the child's colour seeing and word hearing and speaking memories, by which the proper name for the colours is brought up in his mind. 4. Equally ready facility in the pronunciation of the various names of the colours which he recognises; and there is the further embarrassment, that any such process which involves association of ideas, is as varied as the lives of children. The single fact that speech is acquired long after objects and some colours are distinguished, shows that results reached by this method have very little value as far as the problem of the first perception of colours is concerned.

That the fourth element pointed out above is a real source of confusion is shown by the fact that children recognise many words which they can not readily pronounce. When this was realized, a second phase in the development of the problem arose. A colour was named, and then the child was required to pick out that colour. This gave results different from those reached by the first method, blue and red leading the list in correct answers by the first method, while by this second method yellow led, and blue came near the end of the list.

The further objection that colours might be distinguished before the word names are learned, or that colour words might be interchanged or confused by the child, gave rise to what we may call the third stage in the statement of the problem. The method of "recognition" took the place of the method of "naming." This consisted in showing to a child a coloured disk, without naming it, and then asking him to pick out the same colour from a number of coloured disks.

This reduces the question to the second of the four I have named above. It is the usual method of testing for colour blindness, in which, from defects of vision, certain colours can not be perceived at all. It answers very well for colour blindness; for what we really want to learn in the case of a sailor or a signal-man is whether he can recognise a given signal when it is repeated; that is, does he know green or red to be the same as his former experience of green or red? But it is evident that there is still a more fundamental question in the matter--the real question of colour perception. It is quite possible that a child might not recognise an isolated colour when he could really very well distinguish the colours lying side by side. The last question, then, is this: When does the child get the different colour Sensations (not recognitions), and in what order?

To solve this question it would seem that experiments should be made upon younger children. The results described above were all secured after the children had made considerable progress in learning to speak.

To meet this requirement another method may be used which can be applied to children less than a year old. The colours are shown, and the child led to grasp after them. This method is of such a character as to yield a series of experiments whose results are in terms of the most fundamental movements of the infant; it can be easily and pleasantly conducted; and it is of wide application. The child's hand movements are nearly ideal in this respect. The hand reflects the child's first feelings, and becomes the most mobile organ of his volition, except his organs of speech. We find spontaneous arm and hand movements, reflex movements, reaching-out movements, grasping movements, imitative movements, manipulating movements, and voluntary efforts--all these, in order, reflecting the development of the mind.

To illustrate this method, I may cite certain results reached by myself on the questions of colour and distance perception, and right-handedness in the child.

Distance and Colour Perception.--I undertook at the beginning of my child H.'s ninth month to experiment with her with a view to arriving at the exact state of her colour perception, and also to investigate her sense of distance. The arrangements consisted in this instance in giving the infant a comfortable sitting posture, kept constant by a band passing around her chest and fastened securely to the back of her chair. Her arms were left bare and quite free in their movements. Pieces of paper of different colours were exposed before her, at varying distances, front, right, and left. This was regulated by a framework, consisting of a horizontal rod graded in inches, projecting from the back of the chair at a level with her shoulder and parallel with her arm when extended straight forward, and carrying on it another rod, also graded in inches, at right angles to the first. This second rod was thus a horizontal line directly in front of the child, parallel with a line connecting her shoulders, and so equally distant for both hands. This second rod was made to slide upon the first, so as to be adjusted at any desired distance from the child. On this second rod the colours, etc., were placed in succession, the object being to excite the child to reach for them. So far from being distasteful to the infant, I found that, with pleasant suggestions thrown about the experiments, the whole procedure gave her much gratification, and the affair became one of her pleasant daily occupations. After each sitting she was given a reward of some kind. I give the results, both for colour and distance, of 217 experiments. Of these 111 were with five colours and 106 with ordinary newspaper (chosen as a relatively neutral object, which would have no colour value and no association, to the infant).

Colour.--The colours range themselves in the order of attractiveness--blue, red, white, green, and brown. Disregarding white, the difference between blue and red is very slight, compared with that between any other two. This confirms the results of the second method described above. Brown, to my child--as tested in this way--seemed to be about as neutral as could well be. A similar distaste for brown has been noticed by others. White, on the other hand, was more attractive than green. I am sorry that my list did not include yellow. The newspaper was, at reaching distance (9 to 10 inches) and a little more (up to 14 inches), as attractive as the average of the colours, and even as much so as the red; but this is probably due to the fact that the newspaper experiments came after a good deal of practice in reaching after colours, and a more exact association between the stimulus and its distance. At 15 inches and over, the newspaper was refused in 93 per cent of the cases, while blue was refused at that distance in only 75 per cent, and red in 83 per cent.

Distance.--In regard to the question of distance, the child persistently refused to reach for anything put 16 inches or more away from her. At 15 inches she refused 91 per cent of all the cases, 90 per cent of the colour cases, and, as I have said, 93 per cent of the newspaper cases. At nearer distances we find the remarkable uniformity with which the safe-distance association works at this early age. At 14 inches only 14 per cent of all the cases were refused, and at 13 inches only about 7 per cent. There was a larger percentage of refusals at 11 and 12 inches than at 13 and 14 inches, a result due to the influence of the brown, which was refused consistently when more than 10 inches away. The fact that there were no refusals to reach for anything exposed within reaching distance (10 inches)--other attractive objects being kept away--shows two things; (1) the very fine estimation visually of the distance represented by the arm-length; and (2) the great uniformity at this age of the phenomenon of Motor Suggestion upon which this method of child study is based, and which is referred to again below. In respect to the first point, it will be remembered that the child does not begin to reach for anything that it sees until about the fourth or sixth week; so it is evident at what a remarkably fast rate those obscure factors of size, perspective, light and shade, etc., which signify distance to the eye, become associated with arm movements of reaching. This method, applied with proper precautions, obviates many of the difficulties of the others. There are certain requirements of proper procedure, however, which should never be neglected by any one who experiments with young children.

In the first place, the child is peculiarly susceptible to the appeals of change, novelty, chance, or happy suggestion; and often the failure to respond to a stimulus is due to distraction or to discomfort rather than to lack of intrinsic interest. Again, fatigue is a matter of considerable importance. In respect to fatigue, I should say that the first signs of restlessness, or arbitrary loss of interest, in a series of stimulations, is sufficient warning, and all attempts at further experimenting should cease. Often the child is in a state of indisposition, of trifling nervous irritability, etc.; this should be detected beforehand, and then nothing should be undertaken. No series longer than three trials should be attempted without changing the child's position, resting its attention with a song, or a game, etc., and thus leading it fresh to its task again. Furthermore, no single stimulus, as a colour, should be twice repeated without a change to some other, since the child's eagerness or alertness is somewhat satisfied by the first effort, and a new thing is necessary to bring him out to full exercise again. After each effort or two the child should be given the object reached for to hold or play with for a moment; otherwise he grows to apprehend that the whole affair is a case of "Tantalus." In all these matters very much depends upon the knowledge and care of the experimenter, and his ability to keep the child in a normal condition of pleasurable muscular exercise throughout.

In performing colour experiments, several requirements would appear to be necessary for exact results. Should not the colours chosen be equal in purity, intensity, lustre, illumination, etc.? In reference to these differences, I think only that degree of care need be exercised which good comparative judgment provides. Colours of about equal objective intensity, of no gloss, of relatively evident spectral purity, under constant illumination--this is all that is required. The variations due to the grosser factors I have mentioned--such as condition of attention, physical unrest, disturbing noises, sights, etc.--are of greater influence than any of these more recondite variations in the stimulus. Intensity and lustre, however, are certainly important. It is possible, by carefully choosing a room of pretty constant daylight illumination, and setting the experiments at the same hour each day, to secure a regular degree of brightness if the colours themselves are equally bright; and lustre may be ruled out by using coloured wools or blotting-papers. The papers used in the experiments given above were coloured blotting-papers. The omission of yellow is due to the absence, in the neighbourhood, of a satisfactory yellow paper.

The method now described may be further illustrated by the following experiments on the use of the hands by the young child.

The Origin of Right-handedness.--The question, "Why are we right or left-handed?" has exercised the speculative ingenuity of many men. It has come to the front anew in recent years, in view of the advances made in the general physiology of the nervous system; and certainly we are now in a better position to set the problem intelligently and to hope for its solution. Hitherto the actual conditions of the rise of "dextrality" in young children--as the general fact of uneven-handedness may be called--have not been closely observed. It was to gain light, therefore, upon the facts themselves that the experiments described in the following pages were carried out.

My child H. was placed in a comfortable sitting posture, the arms left bare and free in their movement, and allowed to reach for objects placed before her in positions exactly determined and recorded by the simple arrangement of sliding rods already described. The experiments took place at the same hour daily, for a period extending from her fourth to her tenth month. These experiments were planned with very great care and with especial view to the testing of several hypotheses which, although superficial to those who have studied physiology, yet constantly recur in publications on this subject. Among these theories certain may be mentioned with regard to which my experiments were conclusive. It has frequently been held that a child's right-handedness arises from the nurse's or mother's constant method of carrying it, the child's hand which is left free being more exercised, and so becoming stronger. This theory is ambiguous as regards both mother and child. The mother, if right-handed, would carry the child on the left arm, in order to work with the right arm. This I find an invariable tendency with myself and with nurses and mothers whom I have observed. But this would leave the child's left arm free, and so a right-handed mother would be found with a left-handed child! Again, if the mother or nurse be left-handed, the child would tend to be right-handed. Or if, as is the case in civilized countries, nurses largely replace the mothers, it would be necessary that most of the nurses be left-handed in order to make most of the children right-handed. Now, none of these deductions are true. Further, the child, as a matter of fact, holds on with both hands, however it is itself held.

Another theory maintains that the development of right-handedness is due to differences in weight of the two lateral halves of the body; this tends to bring more strain on one side than the other, and to give more exercise, and so more development, to that side. This evidently assumes that children are not right or left-handed before they learn to stand. This my results given below show to be false. Again, we are told that infants get right-handed by being placed on one side too much for sleep; this can be shown to have little force also when the precaution is taken to place the child alternately on its right and left sides for its sleeping periods.

In the case of the child H., certain precautions were carefully enforced. She was never carried about in arms at all, never walked with when crying or sleepless; she was frequently turned over in her sleep; she was not allowed to balance herself on her feet until a later period than that covered by the experiments. Thus the conditions of the rise of the right-handed era were made as simple and uniform as possible.

The experiments included, besides reaching for colours, a great many of reaching for other objects, at longer and shorter distances, and in unsymmetrical directions. I give some details of the results of the experiments in which simple objects were used, extending over a period of four months, from the fifth to the ninth in her life. The number of experiments at each sitting varied from ten to forty, the position of the child being reversed as to light from windows, position of observation, etc., after half of each series.

No trace of preference for either hand was discernible during this period; indeed, the neutrality was as complete as if it had been arranged beforehand, or had followed the throwing of dice.

I then conceived the idea that possibly a severer distance test might affect the result and show a marked preferential response by one hand over the other. I accordingly continued to use a neutral stimulus, but placed it from twelve to fifteen inches away from the child. This resulted in very hard straining on her part, with all the signs of physical effort (explosive breathing sounds resulting from the setting of the larynx, rush of blood to the head, seen in the flushing of the face, etc.). The number of experiments in each series was intentionally made very small, from one to twelve, in order to avoid fatigue.

The results were now very interesting. During the month ending June 15th the child showed no decided preference for either hand in reaching straight before her within the easy reaching distance of ten inches, but a slight balance in favour of the left hand; yet she was right-handed to a marked degree during the same period as regards movements which required effort or strain, such as grasping for objects twelve to fifteen inches distant. For the greater distances, the left hand was used in only five cases as against seventy-four cases of the use of the right hand; and further, all these five cases were twelve-inch distances, the left hand being used absolutely not at all in the forty-five cases at longer distances.

In order to test this further, I varied the point of exposure of the stimulus to the right or left, aiming thus to attract the hand on one side or the other, and so to determine whether the growth of such a preference was limited to experiences of convenience in reaching to adjacent local objects, etc.

The deviation to the left in front of the body only called out the right hand to greater exertion, while the left hand fell into still greater disuse. This seems to show that "dextrality" is not derived from the experience of the individual in using either hand predominantly for reaching, grasping, holding, etc., within the easiest range of that hand. The right hand intruded regularly upon the domain of the left.

Proceeding upon the clew thus obtained, a clew which seems to suggest that the hand preference is influenced by the stimulus to the eye, I introduced hand observations into a series of experiments already mentioned above on the same child's perception of the different colours; thinking that the colour stimulus which represented the strongest inducement to the child to reach might have the same effect in determining the use of the right hand as the increased distance in the experiments already described. This inference is proved to be correct by the results.

It should be added that in all cases in which both hands were used together, each hand was called out with evident independence of the other, both about the same time, and both carried energetically to the goal. In many other cases in which either right or left hand is given in the results, the other hand also moved, but in a subordinate and aimless way. There was a very marked difference between the use of both hands in some cases, and of one hand followed by, or accompanied by, the other in other cases. It was very rare that the second hand did not thus follow or accompany the first; and this was extremely marked in the violent reaching for which the right hand was mainly used. This movement was almost invariably accompanied by an objectless and fruitless symmetrical movement of the other hand.

The results of the entire series of experiments on the use of the hands may be stated as follows, mainly in the words in which they were summarily reported some time ago:

1. I found no continued preference for either hand as long as there were no violent muscular exertions made (based on 2,187 systematic experiments in cases of free movement of hands near the body--i. e., right hand, 577 cases; left hand, 568 cases--a difference of 9 cases; both hands, 1,042 cases; the difference of 9 cases being too slight to have any meaning); the period covered being from the child's sixth to her tenth month inclusive.

2. Under the same conditions, the tendency to use both hands together was about double the tendency to use either (seen from the number of cases of the use of both hands in the figures given above).

3. A distinct preference for the right hand in violent efforts in reaching became noticeable in the seventh and eighth months. Experiments during the eighth month on this cue gave, in 80 cases, right hand, 74 cases; left hand, 5 cases; both hands, 1 case. This was true in two very distinct classes of cases: first, reaching for objects, neutral as regards colour (newspaper, etc.), at more than the reaching distance; and, second, reaching for bright colours at any distance. Under the stimulus of bright colours, from 86 cases, 84 were right-hand cases and 2 left-hand. Right-handedness had accordingly developed under pressure of muscular effort in the sixth and seventh months, and showed itself also under the influence of a strong colour stimulus to the eye.

4. Up to this time the child had not learned to stand or to creep; hence the development of one hand more than the other is not due to differences in weight between the two longitudinal halves of the body. As she had not learned to speak or to utter articulate sounds with much distinctness, we may say also that right or left-handedness may develop while the speech centres are not yet functioning. Further, the right hand is carried over after objects on the left side, showing that habit in reaching does not determine its use.

Theoretical.--Some interesting points arise in connection with the interpretation of these facts. If it be true that the order of rise of mental and physiological functions is constant, then for this question the results obtained in the case of one child, if accurate, would hold for others apart from any absolute time determination. We should expect, therefore, that these results would be confirmed by experiments on other children, and this is the only way their correctness can be tested.

If, when tested, they should be found correct, they would be sufficient answer to several of the theories of right-handedness heretofore urged, as has been already remarked. The rise of the phenomenon must be sought, therefore, in more deep-going facts of physiology than such theories supply. Furthermore, if we go lower in the animal scale than man, analogies for the kinds of experience which are urged as reasons for right-handedness are not present; animals do not carry their young, nor pat them to sleep, nor do animals shake hands!

A full discussion would lead us to the conclusion that dextrality is due to a difference in development in the two hemispheres of the brain, that these differences are hereditary, and that they show themselves toward the end of the first year.

It is a singular circumstance that right-handedness and speech are controlled by the same hemisphere of the brain and from contiguous areas. It would explain this--and at the same time it seems probable from other considerations--if we found that right-handedness was first used for expression before speech; and that speech has arisen from the setting aside, for further development, of the area in the brain first used for right-handedness. Musical expression has its seat in or near the same lobe of the brain.

The Child's Mental Development in General.--The actual development of the child, as observations from many sources indicate it, may be sketched very briefly in its main outlines. It is probable that the earliest consciousness is simply a mass of touch and muscular sensations experienced in part before birth. Shortly after birth the child begins to connect his impressions with one another and to show Memory. But both memory and Association are very weak, and depend upon intense stimulations, such as bright lights, loud noises, etc. The things which most effect him at these early stages are those which bring him into conditions of sharp physical pain or give him acute pleasure. Yet it is a remarkable fact that at birth the pain reflex is wanting. His whole life up to about the fourth month turns upon his organic and vegetative needs. At three months the young child will forget his mother or nurse after a very few days. Attention begins to arise about the end of the first quarter year, appearing first in response to bright lights and loud sounds, and being for a considerable time purely reflex, drawn here and there by the successive impressions which the environment makes. With lights and sounds, however, movements also attract the infant's attention very early; and the passage from reflex attention to a sort of vague interest seems to arise first in connection with the movements of the persons about him. This interest goes on to develop very rapidly in the second half year, in connection more particularly with the movements which are associated with the child's own comfort and discomfort. The association of muscular sensations with those of touch and sight serves to give him his first clear indications of the positions of his own members and of other objects. His discrimination of what belongs to his own body is probably aided by so-called "double touch"--the fact that when he touches his own body, as in touching his foot with the hand, he has two sensations, one in the foot and the other in the hand. This is not the case when he touches other objects, and he soon learns the distinction, getting the outlines of his own body marked out in a vague way. The learning of the localities on his body which he can not see, however, lags far behind. The movements of his limbs in active exploration, accompanied by sight, enables him to build up his knowledge of the world about him. Learning this he soon falls to "experimenting" with the things of space. Thus he begins to find out how things fit together, and what their uses are.

On the side of his movements we find him going through a series of remarkable adaptations to his environment. At the beginning his movements are largely random discharges, or reflexes of an instinctive character, such as sucking. Yet in the first month he shows the beginning of adaptation to the suggestions of his daily life, the first manifestations of acquired Habit. He learns when and how long he is expected to sleep, when and how much to eat; he very soon finds out the peculiar touch and vocal tones of this person or that, and acts upon these distinctions. He gets to know the meaning of his food bottle, to understand the routine movements of persons about the room, and the results of violations of their order. His hat, wraps, carriage, become in the first half year signals to him of the outdoor excursion. He no longer bobs his head about when held erect, and begins to control his natural processes. The remarkable thing about all these adaptations is that they occur before the infant can in any sense be said to have a Will; for, as has been said, the fibres of the brain necessary to voluntary action--in the cortex of the hemispheres--are not yet formed.

The realization of this extraordinary adaptiveness of the very young child should save parents many an anxious day and sleepless night. There is practically nothing more easy than to impress upon the child whatever habits of daily--and nightly!--routine one wishes to give him, if he be taken early enough. The only requirements are knowledge of what is good for him, and then inviolable regularity in everything that concerns him. Under this treatment he will become as "obstinate" in being "good" as the opposite so-called indulgent or capricious treatment always make him in being "bad." There is no reason whatever that he should be walked with or held, that he should be taken up when he cries, that he should be trotted when he awakes, or that he should have a light by night. Things like this are simply bad habits for which the parents have themselves to thank. The child adapts himself to his treatment, and it is his treatment that his habits reflect.

During the second half-year--sooner or later in particular cases--the child is ready to begin to imitate. Imitation is henceforth, for the following few years, the most characteristic thing about his action. He first imitates movements, later sounds, especially vocal sounds. His imitations themselves also show progress, being at first what is called "simple imitation" (repeating a distinction already spoken of in the chapter on animals), as when the child lies in bed in the morning and repeats the same sound over and over again. He hears his own voice and imitates it. In this sort of imitation he simply allows his instinct to reproduce what he hears without control or interference from him. He does not improve, but goes on making the same sounds with the same mistakes again and again. But a little later he begins what is called "persistent imitation"--the "try-try-again," already spoken of--which is a very different thing. Persistent imitation shows unmistakably the presence of will. The child is not satisfied with simple imitation or mere repetition, whether it be good or bad in its results. He now sees his errors and aims consciously to improve. Note the child's struggles to speak a word right by imitation of the pronunciation of others. And he succeeds. He gradually gets his muscles under control by persistence in his try-try-again.

Then he goes further--about the beginning of his second year, usually. He gets the idea that imitation is the way to learn, and turns all his effort into imitations experimentally carried out. He is now ready to learn most of the great processes of his later culture. Speech, writing, this special accomplishment and that, are all learned by experimental imitation.

The example of the child's trying to draw or write has already been cited. He looks at the copy before him; sets all his muscles of hand and arm into massive contraction; turns and twists his tongue, bends his body, winds his legs together, holds his breath, and in every way concentrates his energies upon the copying of the model. In all this he is experimenting.

He produces a wealth of movements, from which, very gradually, as he tries and tries again, the proper ones are selected out. These he practises, and lets the superfluous ones fall away, until he secures the requisite control over hand and arm. Or suppose a child endeavouring, in the crudest fashion, to put a rubber on the end of a pencil, after seeing some one else do it--just the sort of thing a year-old child loves to imitate. What a chaos of ineffective movements! But with repeated effort he gets nearer and nearer to it, and finally succeeds.

On the side of action, two general principles have been formulated in child psychology, both illustrated in the cases and experiments now given: The one, Motor Suggestion, is, as we saw, a principle of general psychology. Its importance to the child is that by it he forms Habits, useful responses to his environment, and so saves himself many sad blunders. The other principle is that of Imitation; by it the child learns new things directly in the teeth of his habits. By exercising in an excessive way what he has already learned through his experimental imitations, he is continually modifying his habits and making new adaptations. These two principles dominate the active life of the adult man as well.

Personality Suggestion.--A further set of facts may be cited to illustrate the working of Suggestion, now in the sphere of the receptive life. They are important as showing the child's progress in learning the great features of personality.

One of the most remarkable tendencies of the very young child in its responses to its environment is the tendency to recognise differences of personality. It responds to what have been called Suggestions of Personality. As early as the second month it distinguishes its mother's or nurse's touch in the dark. It learns characteristic methods of holding, taking up, patting, kissing, etc., and adapts itself, by a marvellous accuracy of protestation or acquiescence, to these personal variations. Its associations of personality come to be of such importance that for a long time its happiness or misery depends upon the presence of certain kinds of "personality suggestion." It is quite a different thing from the child's behavior toward things which are not persons. Things come to be, with some few exceptions which are involved in the direct gratification of appetite, more and more unimportant; things may be subordinated to regular treatment or reaction. But persons become constantly more important, as uncertain and dominating agents of pleasure and pain. The sight of movement by persons, with its effects on the infant, seems to be the most important factor in this peculiar influence; later the voice comes to stand for a person's presence, and at last the face and its expressions equal the person in all his attributes.

I think this distinction between persons and things, between agencies and objects, is the child's very first step toward a sense of personality. The sense of uncertainty or lack of confidence grows stronger and stronger in his dealings with persons--an uncertainty aroused by the moods, emotions, changes of expression, and shades of treatment of the persons around it. A person stands for a group of quite unstable experiences. This period we may, for brevity of expression, assuming it to be first in order of development, call the "projective" stage in the growth of the child's personal consciousness.

It is from this beginning that the child goes on to become fully conscious of what persons are. And when we observe his actions more closely we find no less than four steps in his growth, which, on account of the importance of the topic, may be stated in some little detail.

1. The first thing of significance to him, as has been said, is movement. The first attempts of the infant at anything like steady attention are directed to moving things--a swaying curtain, a moving light, a stroking touch, etc. And further than this, the moving things soon become more than objects of curiosity; these things are just the things that affect him with pleasure or pain.

It is movement that brings him his bottle, movement that regulates the stages of his bath, movement that dresses him comfortably, movement that sings to him and rocks him to sleep. In that complex of sensations, the nurse, the feature of importance to him, of immediate satisfaction or redemption from pain, is this--movements come to succour him. Change in his bodily feeling is the vital requirement of his life, for by it the rhythm of his vegetative existence is secured; and these things are accompanied and secured always in the moving presence of the one he sees and feels about him. This, I take it, is the earliest reflection in his consciousness of the world of personalities about him. At this stage his "personality suggestion" is a pain-movement-pleasure state of mind; to this he reacts with a smile, and a crow, and a kick. Undoubtedly this association gets some of its value from the other similar one in which the movements are the infant's own. It is by movements that he gets rid of pains and secures pleasures.

Many facts tend to bear out this position. My child cried in the dark when I handled her, although I imitated the nurse's movements as closely as possible. She tolerated a strange presence so long as it remained quietly in its place; but let it move, and especially let it usurp any of the pieces of movement-business of the nurse or mother, and her protests were emphatic. The movements tended to bring the strange elements of a new face into the vital association, pain-movement-pleasure, and so to disturb its familiar course; this constituted it a strange "personality."

It is astonishing, also, what new accidental elements may become parts of this association. Part of a movement, a gesture, a peculiar habit of the nurse, may become sufficient to give assurance of the welcome presence and the pleasures which the presence brings. Two notes of my song in the night stood for my presence to H., and no song from any one else could replace it. A lighted match stopped the crying of E. for food in her fourteenth week, although it was but a signal for a process of food preparation lasting several minutes; and a simple light never stopped her crying under any other circumstances.

2. With this first start in the sense of personality we find also the beginning of the recognition of different personalities. It is evident that the sense of another's presence thus felt in the infant's consciousness rests, as all associations rest, upon regularity or repetition; his sense of expectancy is

aroused whenever the chain of events is started. This is soon embodied largely in two indications: the face and the voice. But it is easy to see that this is a very meagre sense of personality; a moving machine which brought pain and alleviated suffering might serve as well. So the child begins to learn, in addition, the fact that persons are in a measure individual in their treatment of him; that their individuality has elements of uncertainty or irregularity about it. This growing sense is very clear to one who watches an infant in its second half year. Sometimes its mother gives it a biscuit, but sometimes she does not. Sometimes the father smiles and tosses the child; sometimes he does not. Even the indulgence of the grandmother has its times and seasons. The child looks for signs of these varying moods and methods of treatment; for his pains of disappointment arise directly on the basis of that former sense of regular personal presence upon which his expectancy goes forth.

This new element of the child's sense of persons becomes, at one period of its development, quite the controlling element. His action in the presence of the persons of the household becomes hesitating and watchful. Especially does he watch the face, for any expressive indications of what treatment is to be expected; for facial expression is now the most regular as well as the most delicate indication. Special observations on H.'s responses to changes in facial expression up to the age of twenty months showed most subtle sensibility to these differences; and normal children all do. Animals are also very expert at this.

All through the child's second year, and longer, his sense of the persons around him is in this stage. The incessant "why?" with which he greets any action affecting him, or any information given him, is witness to the simple puzzle of the apparent capriciousness of persons. Of course he can not understand "why"; so the simple fact to him is that mamma will or won't, he knows not beforehand which. He is unable to anticipate the treatment in detail, and he has not of course learned any principles of interpretation of the conduct of father or mother lying back of the details.

But in all this period there is germinating in his consciousness--and this very uncertainty is an important element of it--the seed of a far-reaching thought. His sense of persons--moving, pleasure-or-pain-giving, uncertain but self-directing persons--is now to become a sense of agency, of power, which is yet not the power of the regular-moving door on its hinges or the rhythmic swinging of the pendulum of the clock. The sense of personal agency is now forming, and it again is potent for still further development of the social consciousness. It is just here, I think, that imitation becomes so important in the child's life. This is imitation's opportunity. The infant watches to see how others act, because his own weal and woe depends upon this "how"; and inasmuch as he knows not what to anticipate, his mind is open to every suggestion of movement. So he falls to imitating. His attention dwells upon details, and by the principle of adaptation which imitation expresses, it acts out these details for himself.

It is an interesting detail, that at this stage the child begins to grow capricious himself; to feel that he can do whatever he likes. Suggestion begins to lose the regularity of its working, for it meets the child's growing sense of his own agency. The youthful hero becomes "contrary." At this period it is that obedience begins to grow hard, and its meaning begins to dawn upon the child as the great reality. For it means the subjection of his own agency, his own liberty to be capricious, to the agency and liberty of some one else.

3. With all this, the child's distinction between and among the persons who constantly come into contact with him grows on apace, in spite of the element of irregularity of the general fact of personality. As he learned before the difference between one presence and another, so now he learns the difference between one character and another. Every character is more or less regular in its irregularity. It has its tastes and modes of action, its temperament and type of command. This the child learns late in the second year and thereafter. He behaves differently when the father is in the room. He is quick to obey one person, slow to obey another. He cries aloud, pulls his companions, and behaves reprehensibly generally, when no adult is present who has authority or will to punish him. This stage in his "knowledge of man" leads to very marked differences of conduct on his part.

4. He now goes on to acquire real self-consciousness and social feeling. This stage is so important that we may give to it a separate heading below.

It may not be amiss to sum up what has been said about Personality-Suggestion. It is a general term for the information which the child gets about persons. It develops through three or four roughly distinguished stages, all of which illustrate what is called the "projective" sense of personality.[2] There is, 1. A bare distinction of persons from things on the ground of peculiar pain-movement-pleasure experiences. 2. A sense of the irregularity or capriciousness of the behaviour of these persons, which suggests personal agency. 3. A distinction, vaguely felt perhaps, but wonderfully reflected in the child's actions, between the modes of behaviour or personal characters of different persons. 4. After his sense of his own agency arises by the process of imitation, he gets what is really self-consciousness and social feeling.

[Footnote 2: It is very remarkable that in the child's bashfulness we find a native nervous response to the presence of persons. And it is curious to note that, besides the general gregariousness which many animals have, they show in many instances special responses of the presence of creatures of their own kind or of other kinds. Dogs seem to recognise dogs by smell. So with cats, which also respond instinctively with strong repulsion to the smell of dogs. Horses seem to be guided by sight. Fowls are notoriously blind to shapes of fowls, but depend on hearing the cries of their kind or their young.]

Self-consciousness.--So far as we have now gone the child has only a very dim distinction between himself as a person and the other persons who move about him. The persons are "projective" to him, mere bodies or external objects of a peculiar sort classed together because they show common marks. Yet in the sense of agency, he has already begun, as we saw, to find in himself a mental nucleus, or centre. This comes about from his tendency to fall into the imitation of the acts of others.

Now as he proceeds with these imitations of others, he finds himself gradually understanding the others, by coming, through doing the same actions with them, to discover what they are feeling, what their motives are, what the laws of their behaviour. For example, he sees his father handle a pin, then suddenly make a face as he pricks himself, and throws the pin away. All this is simply a puzzle to the child; his father's conduct is capricious, "projective." But the child's curiosity in the matter takes the form of imitation; he takes up the pin himself and goes through the same manipulation of it that his father did. Thus he gets himself pricked, and with it has the impulse to throw the pin away. By imitating his father he has now discovered what was inside the father's mind, the pain and the motive of the action.

This way of proceeding in reference to the actions of others, of which many examples might be given, has a twofold significance in the development of the child; and because of this twofold significance it is one of the most important facts of psychology. Upon it rest, in the opinion of the present writer, correct views of ethics and social philosophy.

1. By such imitation the child learns to associate his own sense of physical power, together with his own private pleasures and pains, with the personal actions which were before observed, it is true, in other persons but not understood. The act of the father has now become his own. So one by one the various attributes which he has found to be characteristic of the persons of his social circle, become his, in his own thought. He is now for himself an agent who has the marks of a Person or a Self. He now understands from the inside all the various personal suggestions. What he saw persons do is now no longer "projective"--simply there, outside, in the environment; it has become what we call "subjective." The details are grouped and held together by the sense of agency working itself out in his imitative struggles.

This is what we mean by Self-consciousness. It is not an inborn thing with the child. He gradually acquires it. And it is not a sense of a distinct and separate self, first known and then compared with other persons. On the contrary, it is gradually built up in the child's mind from the same material exactly as that of which he makes up his thought of other persons. The deeds he can do he first sees others doing; only then can he imitate them and find out that he also is a being who can perform them.

So it goes all through our lives. Our sense of Self is constantly changing, constantly being enriched. We have not the same thought of self two days in succession. To-day I think of myself as something to be proud of, to-morrow as something to be ashamed of. To-day I learn something from you, and the thought that it is common to you and to me is the basis of my sympathy with you. To-morrow I learn to commit the unworthy act which Mr. A. commits, and the thought that he and I are so far the same is the basis of the common disapproval which I feel of him and me.

2. The second result of this imitative learning about personality is of equal importance. When the child has taken up an action by imitation and made it subjective, finding out that personality has an inside, something more than the mere physical body, then he reads this fact back into the other persons

also. He says to himself: "He too, my little brother, must have in him a sense of agency similar to this of mine. He acts imitatively, too; he has pleasures and pains; he shows sympathy for me, just as I do for him. So do all the persons with whom I have become so far acquainted. They are, then, 'subjects' as I am--something richer than the mere 'projects' which I had supposed." So other persons become essentially like himself; and not only like himself, but identical with himself so far as the particular marks are concerned which he has learned from them. For it will be remembered that all these marks were at first actually taken up by imitation from these very persons. The child is now giving back to his parents, teachers, etc., only the material which he himself took from them. He has enriched it, to be sure; with it he now reads into the other persons the great fact of subjective agency; but still whatever he thinks of them has come by way of his thought of himself, and that in turn was made up from them.

This view of the other person as being the same in the main as the self who thinks of the other person, is what psychologists mean when they speak of the "ejective" self. It is the self of some one else as I think of it; in other words, it is myself "ejected" out by me and lodged in him.

The Social and Ethical Sense.--From this we see what the Social Sense is. It is the feeling which arises in the child or man of the real identity, through its imitative origin, of all possible thoughts of self, whether yourself, myself, or some one else's self. The bond between you and me is not an artificial one; it is as natural as is the recognition of personal individuality. And it is doing violence to this fundamental fact to say, as social science so often assumes, that the individual naturally separates himself or his interests from the self or the interests of others. He is, on the contrary, bound up with others from the start by the very laws of his growth. His social action and feeling are natural to him. The child can not be selfish only nor generous only; he may seem to be this or that, in this circumstance or that, but he is really social all the time.

Furthermore, his sense of right and wrong, his Ethical Sense, grows up upon this sense of the social bond. This I can not stop to explain further. But it is only when social relationships are recognised as essential in the child's growth that we can understand the mutual obligations and duties which the moral life imposes upon us all.

How to Observe Children, with Especial Reference to Observations of Imitation.--There are one or two considerations of such practical importance to all those who wish to observe children that I venture to throw them together--only saying, by way of introduction, that nothing less than the child's personality is at stake in the method and matter of its imitations. The Self is really the form in which the personal influences surrounding the child take on their new individuality.

1. No observations are of much importance which are not accompanied by a detailed statement of the personal influences which have affected the child. This is the more important since the child sees few persons, and sees them constantly. It is not only likely--it is inevitable--that he make up his personality, under limitations of heredity, by imitation, out of the "copy" set in the actions, temper, emotions, of the persons who build around him the social enclosure of his childhood. It is only necessary to watch a two-year-old closely to see what members of the family are giving him his personal "copy"--to find out whether he sees his mother constantly and his father seldom; whether he plays much with other children, and what in some degree their dispositions are; whether he is growing to be a person of subjection, equality, or tyranny; whether he is assimilating the elements of some low unorganized social personality from his foreign nurse. The boy or girl is a social "monad," to use Leibnitz's figure in a new context, a little world, which reflects the whole system of influences coming to stir his sensibility. And just in so far as his sensibilities are stirred, he imitates, and forms habits of imitating; and habits?--they are character!

2. A point akin to the first is this: the observation of each child should describe with great accuracy the child's relations to other children. Has he brothers or sisters? how many of each, and of what age? Does he sleep in the same bed or room with them? Do they play much with one another alone? The reason is very evident. An only child has only adult "copy." He can not interpret his father's actions, or his mother's, oftentimes. He imitates very blindly. He lacks the more childish example of a brother or sister near himself in age. And this difference is of very great importance to his development. He lacks the stimulus, for example, of games in which personification is a direct tutor to selfhood, as I shall remark further on. And while he becomes precocious in some lines of instruction, he fails in variety of imagination, in richness of fancy, at the same time that his imaging processes are more wild

and uncontrolled. The dramatic, in his sense of social situations, is largely hidden. It is a very great mistake to isolate children, especially to separate off one or two children. One alone is perhaps the worse, but two alone are subject to the other element of social danger which I may mention next.

3. Observers should report with especial care all cases of unusually close relationship between children in youth, such as childish favoritism, "platonic friendships," "chumming," in school or home, etc. We have in these facts-- and there is a very great variety of them--an exaggeration of the social or imitative tendency, a narrowing down of the personal sensibility to a peculiar line of well-formed influences. It has never been studied by writers either on the genesis of social emotion or on the practice of education. To be sure, teachers have been alive to the pros and cons of allowing children and students to room together; but that has been with view to the possibility of direct immoral or unwholesome contagion. This danger is certainly real; but we, as psychological observers, and above all as teachers and leaders of our children, must go deeper than that. Consider, for example, the possible influence of a school chum and roommate upon a girl in her teens; for this is only an evident case of what all isolated children are subject to. A sensitive nature, a girl whose very life is a branch of a social tree, is placed in a new environment, to engraft upon the members of her mutilated self--her very personality; it is nothing less than that--utterly new channels of supply. The only safety possible, the only way to conserve the lessons of her past, apart from the veriest chance, and to add to the structure of her present character, lies in securing for her the greatest possible variety of social influences. Instead of this, she is allowed to meet, eat, walk, talk, lie down at night, and rise in the morning, with one other person, a "copy" set before her, as immature in all likelihood as herself, or, if not so, yet a single personality, put there to wrap around her growing self the confining cords of unassimilated and foreign habit. Above all things, fathers, mothers, teachers, elders, give the children room! They need all that they can get, and their personalities will grow to fill it. Give them plenty of companions, fill their lives with variety; variety is the soul of originality, and its only source of supply. The ethical life itself, the boy's, the girl's, conscience, is born in the stress of the conflicts of suggestion, born right out of his imitative hesitations; and just this is the analogy which he must assimilate and depend upon in his own conflicts for self-control and social continence. So impressively true is this from the human point of view that, in my opinion--formed, it is true, from the very few

data accessible on such points, still a positive opinion--friendships of a close exclusive kind should be discouraged or broken up, except when under the immediate eye of the wise parent or guardian; and even when allowed, these relationships should, in all cases, be used to entrain the sympathetic and moral sentiments into a wider field of social exercise.

One of the merits of the great English schools and of the free schools of America is that in them the boys acquire, from necessity, the independence of sturdy character, and the self-restraint which is self-imposed. The youth brought up to mind a tutor often fails of the best discipline.

4. The remainder of this section may be devoted to the further emphasis of the need of close observation of children's games, especially those which may be best described as "society games." All those who have given even casual observation to the doings of the nursery have been impressed with the extraordinary facility of the child's mind, from the second year onward, in imagining and plotting social and dramatic situations. It has not been so evident, however, to these casual observers, nor to many really more skilled, that they were observing in these fancy plays the putting together anew of fragments, or larger pieces, of the adult's mental history. Here, in these games, we see the actual use which our children make of the personal "copy" material which they get from you and me. If a man study these games patiently in his own children, and analyze them out, he gradually sees emerge from within the inner consciousness a picture of the boy's own father, whom he aspires to be like, and whose actions he seeks to generalize and apply. The picture is poor, for the child takes only what he is sensible to. And it does seem often, as Sighele pathetically notices on a large social scale, and as the Westminster divines have urged without due sense of the pathetic and home-coming point of it, that he takes more of the bad in us for reproduction than of the good! But, be this as it may, what we give him is all he gets. Heredity does not stop with birth; it is then only beginning. And the pity of it is that this element of heredity, this reproduction of the fathers in the children, which might be used to redeem the new-forming personality from the heritage of past commonness or impurity, is simply left to take its course for the further establishing and confirmation of it. Was there ever a group of school children who did not leave the real school to make a play school, setting up a box for one of their number to sit on and "take off" the teacher? Was there ever a child who did not play "church," and force the improvised

"papa" into the pulpit? Were there ever children who did not "buy" things from fancied stalls in every corner of the nursery, after they had once seen an elder drive a trade in the market? The point is this: the child's personality grows; growth is always by action; he clothes upon himself the scenes of the parent's life and acts them out; so he grows in what he is, what he understands, and what he is able to perform.

In order to be of more direct service to observers of games of this character, let me give a short account of an observation of the kind made some time ago--one of the simplest of many actual situations which my two little girls, Helen and Elizabeth, have acted out together. It is a very commonplace case, a game the elements of which are evident in their origin; but I choose this rather than one more complex, since observers are usually not psychologists, and they find the elementary the more instructive.

On May 2 I was sitting on the porch alone with the children--the two mentioned above, aged respectively four and a half and two and a half years. Helen, the elder, told Elizabeth that she was her little baby; that is, Helen became "mamma," and Elizabeth the "baby." The younger responded by calling her sister "mamma," and the play began.

"You have been asleep, baby. Now it is time to get up," said mamma. Baby rose from the floor--first falling down in order to rise!--was seized upon by "mamma," taken to the railing to an imaginary washstand, and her face washed by rubbing. Her articles of clothing were then named in imagination, and put on, one by one, in the most detailed and interesting fashion. During all this "mamma" kept up a stream of baby talk to her infant: "Now your stockings, my darling; now your skirt, sweetness--O! no--not yet--your shoes first," etc., etc. Baby acceded to all the details with more than the docility which real infants usually show. When this was done--"Now we must go tell papa good-morning, dearie," said mamma. "Yes, mamma," came the reply; and hand in hand they started to find papa. I, the spectator, carefully read my newspaper, thinking, however, that the reality of papa, seeing that he was so much in evidence, would break in upon the imagined situation. But not so. Mamma led her baby directly past me to the end of the piazza, to a column in the corner. "There's papa," said mamma; "now tell him good-morning."-- "Good-morning, papa; I am very well," said baby, bowing low to the column. "That's good," said mamma, in a gruff, low voice, which caused in the real papa a thrill of amused self-consciousness most difficult to contain. "Now you must have your breakfast," said mamma. The seat of a chair was made a breakfast table, the baby's feigned bib put on, and her porridge carefully administered, with all the manner of the nurse who usually directs their breakfast. "Now" (after the meal, which suddenly became dinner instead of breakfast), "you must take your nap," said mamma. "No, mamma; I don't want to," said baby. "But you must."--"No; you be baby, and take the nap."--"But all the other children have gone to sleep, dearest, and the doctor says you must," said mamma. This convinced baby, and she lay down on the floor. "But I haven't undressed you." So then came all the detail of undressing; and mamma carefully covered her up on the floor with a light shawl, saying: "Spring is coming now; that'll be enough. Now shut your eyes, and go to sleep."--"But you haven't kissed me, mamma," said the little one. "Oh, of course, my darling!"--so a long siege of kissing! Then baby closed her eyes very tight, while mamma went on tiptoe away to the end of the porch. "Don't go away, mamma," said baby. "No; mamma wouldn't leave her darling," came the reply.

So this went on. The nap over, a walk was proposed, hats put on, etc., the mamma exercising great care and solicitude for her baby. One further incident to show this: when the baby's hat was put on--the real hat--mamma tied the strings rather tight. "Oh! you hurt, mamma," said baby. "No; mamma wouldn't draw the strings too tight. Let mamma kiss it. There, is that better, my darling?"--all comically true to a certain sweet maternal tenderness which I had no difficulty in tracing.

Now in such a case what is to be reported, of course, is the facts. Yet knowledge of more than the facts is necessary, as I have said above, in order to get the full psychological lesson. We need just the information which concerns the rest of the family and the social influences of the children's lives. I recognised at once every phrase which the children used in this play, where they got it, what it meant in its original context, and how far its meaning had been modified in this process, called in a figure "social heredity." But as that story is reported to strangers who have no knowledge of the children's social antecedents, how much beyond the mere facts of imitation and personification do they get from it? And how much the more is this true when we examine those complex games of the nursery which show the brilliant fancy for situation and drama of the wide-awake four-year-old?

Yet we psychologists are free to interpret; and how rich the lessons even from such a simple scene as this! As for Helen, what could be a more direct lesson--a lived-out exercise--in sympathy, in altruistic self-denial, in the healthy elevation of her sense of self to the dignity of kindly offices, in the sense of responsibility and agency, in the stimulus to original effort and the designing of means to ends--and all of it with the best sense of the objectivity which is quite lost in wretched self-consciousness in us adults, when we personate other characters? What could further all this highest mental growth better than the game by which the lessons of her mother's daily life are read into the child's little self? Then, in the case of Elizabeth also, certain things appear. She obeys without command or sanction, she takes in from her sister the elements of personal suggestion in their simpler childish forms. Certainly such scenes, repeated every day with such variation of detail, must give something of the sense of variety and social equality which real life afterward confirms and proceeds upon; and lessons of the opposite character are learned by the same process.

All this exercise of fancy must strengthen the imaginative faculty also. The prolonged situations, maintained sometimes whole days, or possibly weeks, give strength to the imagination and train the attention. I think, also, that the sense of essential reality, and its distinction from the unreal, the merely imagined, is helped by this sort of symbolic representation. Play has its dangers also--very serious ones. The adults sometimes set bad examples. The game gives practise in cunning no less than in forbearance. Possibly the best service of observation just now is to gather the facts with a view to the proper recognition and avoidance of the dangers.

Finally, I may be allowed a word to interested parents. You can be of no use whatever to psychologists--to say nothing of the actual damage you may be to the children--unless you know your babies through and through. Especially the fathers! They are willing to study everything else. They know every corner of the house familiarly, and what is done in it, except the nursery. A man labours for his children ten hours a day, gets his life insured for their support after his death, and yet he lets their mental growth, the formation of their characters, the evolution of their personality, go on by absorption--if no worse--from common, vulgar, imported and changing, often immoral attendants! Plato said the state should train the children; and added that the wisest man should rule the state. This is to say that the wisest man should tend his children! Hugo gives us, in Jean Valjean and Cosette, a picture of the true paternal relationship. We hear a certain group of studies called the humanities, and it is right. But the best school in the humanities for every man is in his own house.

With this goes, finally, the highest lesson of sport, drama, make-believe, even when we trace it up into the art-impulse--the lesson of personal freedom. The child himself sets the limitations of the game, makes the rules, and subjects himself to them, and then in time pierces the bubble for himself, saying, "I will play no more." All this is the germ of self-regulation, of the control of the impulses, of the voluntary adoption of the ideal, which becomes in later life--if so be that he cling to it--the pearl of great price.

CHAPTER V.

THE CONNECTION OF BODY WITH MIND--PHYSIOLOGICAL PSYCHOLOGY-- MENTAL DISEASES.

In the foregoing pages we have had intimations of some of the important questions which arise about the connection of mind with body. The avenues of the senses are the normal approaches to the mind through the body; and, taking advantage of this, experiments are made upon the senses. This gives rise to Experimental Psychology, to which the chapter after this is devoted. Besides this, however, we find the general fact that a normal body must in all cases be present with a normal mind, and this makes it possible to arrange so to manipulate the body that changes may be produced in the mind in other ways than through the regular channels of sense. For example, we influence the mind when we drink too much tea or coffee, not to mention the greater changes of the same kind which are produced in the mind of the drinker of too much alcohol or other poisonous substances. All the methodical means of procedure by which the psychologist produces effects of this kind by changing the condition or functions of the body within itself belong to Physiological Psychology. So he modifies the respiration, changes the heart beat, stimulates or slows the circulation of the blood, paralyzes the muscles, etc. The ways of procedure may be classified under a few heads, each called a method.

1. Method of Extirpation.--This means simply the cutting away of a part of the body, so that any effect which the loss of the part makes upon the mind may be noted. It is used especially upon the brain. Pieces of the brain, great or small--indeed, practically the whole brain mass--may be removed in many animals without destroying life. Either of the cerebral hemispheres entire, together with large portions of the other, may be taken from the human brain without much effect upon the vital processes, considered as a whole; the actual results being the loss of certain mental functions, such as sight, hearing, power of movement of particular limbs, etc., according to the location of the part which is removed. Many of the facts given below under the heading of Localization were discovered in this way, the guiding principle being that if the loss of a function follows the removal of a certain piece of the brain, then that portion of the brain is directly concerned in the healthy performance of that function.

2. Method of Artificial Stimulation.--As the term indicates, this method proceeds by finding some sort of agent by which the physiological processes may be started artificially; that is, without the usual normal starting of these processes. For example, the physician who stimulates the heart by giving digitalis pursues this method. For psychological purposes this method has also been fruitful in studying the brain, and electricity is the agent customarily used. The brain is laid bare by removing part of the skull of the animal, and the two electrodes of a battery are placed upon a particular point of the brain whose function it is wished to determine. The current passes out along the nerves which are normally set in action from this particular region, and movements of the muscles follow in certain definite parts and directions. This is an indication of the normal function of the part of the brain which is stimulated.

Besides this method of procedure a new one, also by brain stimulation, has recently been employed. It consists in stimulating a spot of the brain as before, but instead of observing the character of the movement which follows, the observer places galvanometers in connection with various members of the body and observes in which of the galvanometers the current comes out of the animal's body (the galvanometer being a very delicate instrument for indicating the presence of an electric current). In this way it is determined along what pathways and to what organs the ordinary vital stimulation passes from the brain, provided it be granted that the electric current takes the same course.

3. Method of Intoxication, called the "Toxic Method."--The remarks above may suffice for a description of this method. The results of the administration of toxic or poisonous agents upon the mind are so general and serious in their character, as readers of De Quincy know, that very little precise knowledge has been acquired by their use.

4. Method of Degeneration.--This consists in observing the progress of natural or artificially produced disease or damage to the tissues, mainly the nervous tissues, with a view to discovering the directions of pathways and the locations of connected functions. The degeneration or decay following disease or injury follows the path of normal physiological action, and so discloses it to the observer. This method is of importance to psychology as affording a means of locating and following up the course of a brain injury which accompanies this or that mental disease or defect.

Results--Localization of Brain Functions.--The more detailed results of this sort of study, when considered on the side of the nervous organism, may be thrown together under the general head of Localization. The greatest result of all is just the discovery that there is such a thing as localization in the nervous system of the different mental functions of sensation and movement. We find particular parts of the nervous organism contributing each its share, in a more or less independent way, to the whole flow of the mental life; and in cases of injury or removal of this part or that, there is a corresponding impairment of the mind.

First of all, it is found that the nervous system has a certain up-and-down arrangement from the segments of the spinal cord up to the gray matter of the rind or "cortex" of the large masses or hemispheres in the skull, to which the word brain is popularly applied. This up-and-down arrangement shows three so-called "levels" of function. Beginning with the spinal cord, we find the simplest processes, and they grow more complex as we go up toward the brain.

The lowest, or "third level," includes all the functions which the spinal cord, and its upper termination, called the "medulla," are able to perform alone-- that is, without involving necessarily the activity of the nervous centres and brain areas which lie above them. Such "third-level" functions are those of the life-sustaining processes generally: breathing, heart-beat, vasomotor action (securing the circulation of the blood), etc. These are all called Automatic processes. They go regularly on from day to day, being constantly stimulated by the normal changes in the physiological system itself, and having no need of interference from the mind of the individual.

In addition to the automatic functions, there is a second great class of processes which are also managed from the third level; that is, by the discharge of nervous energy from particular parts of the spinal cord. These are the so-called Reflex functions. They include all those responses which the nervous system makes to stimulations from the outside, in which the mind has no alternative or control. They happen whether or no. For example, when an object comes near the eye the lid flies to reflexly. If a tap be made upon the knee while one sits with the legs crossed the foot flies up reflexly. Various reflexes may be brought out in a sleeper by slight stimulations to this or that region of his body. Furthermore, each of the senses has its own set of reflex adjustments to the stimulations which come to it. The eye accommodates itself in the most delicate way to the intensity of the light, the distance of the object, the degree of elevation, and the angular displacement of what one looks at. The taking of food into the mouth sets up all sorts of reflex movements which do not cease until the food is safely lodged in the stomach, and so on through a series of physiological adaptations which are simply marvellous in their variety and extent. These processes belong to the third level; and it may surprise the uninitiated to know that not only is the mind quite "out of it" so far as these functions are concerned, but that the brain proper is "out of it" also. Most of these reflexes not only go on when the brain is removed from the skull, but it is an interesting detail that they are generally exaggerated under these conditions. This shows that while the third or lowest level does its own work, it is yet in a sense under the weight--what physiologists call the inhibiting action--of the higher brain masses. It is not allowed to magnify its part too much, nor to work out of its proper time and measure. The nervous apparatus involved in these "third-level" functions may be called the "reflex circuit" (see Fig. 2), the path being from the sense organ up to the centre by a "sensory" nerve, and then out by a "motor" nerve to the muscle.

Going upward in the nervous system, we next find a certain group of bodies within the gross mass of the brain, certain centres lying between the hemispheres above and the medulla and spinal cord below, and in direct connection by nervous tracts with both of these. The technical names of the more important of these organs are these: the "corpora striata," or striped bodies, of which there are two, the "optic thalami," also two in number, and the "cerebellum" or little brain, situated behind. These make up what is called the "second level" in the system. They seem to be especially concerned with the life of sensation. When the centres lying above them, the hemispheres, are removed, the animal is still able to see, hear, etc., and still able to carry out his well-knit habits of action in response to what he sees and hears. But that is about all. A bird treated thus, for example, these second-level centres being still intact while the hemispheres are removed, retains his normal appearance, being quite able to stand upon his feet, to fly, walk, etc. His reflexes are also unimpaired and his inner physiological processes; but it soon becomes noticeable that his mental operations are limited very largely to sensations. He sees his food as usual, but does not remember its use, and makes no attempt to eat it. He sees other birds, but does not respond to their advances. He seems to have forgotten all his education, to have lost all the meanings of things, to have practically no intelligence. A dog in this condition no longer fears the whip, no longer responds to his name, no longer steals food. On the side of his conduct we find that all the actions which he had learned by training now disappear; the trick dog loses all his tricks. What was called Apperception in the earlier chapter seems to have been taken away with the hemispheres.

Coming to the "first level," the highest of all, both in anatomical position and in the character of the functions over which it presides, we see at once what extraordinary importance it has. It comprises the cortex of the hemispheres, which taken together are called the cerebrum. It consists of the parts which we supposed cut out of the pigeon and dog just mentioned; and when we remember what these animals lose by its removal, we see what the normal animal or man owes to the integrity of this organ. It is above all the organ of mind. If we had to say that the mind as such is located anywhere, we should say in the gray matter of the cortex of the hemispheres of the brain. For although, as we saw, animals without this organ can still see and hear and feel, yet we also saw that they could do little else and could learn to do nothing more. All the higher operations of mind come back only when we think of the animal as having normal brain hemispheres.

Further, we find this organ in some degree duplicating the function of the second-level centres, for fibres go out from these intermediate masses to certain areas of the hemispheres, which reproduce locally the senses of hearing, sight, etc. By these fibres the functions of the senses are "projected" out to the surface of the brain, and the term "projection fibres" is applied to the nerves which make these connections. The hemispheres are not content even with the most important of all functions--the strictly intelligent--but they are jealous, so to speak, of the simple sensations which the central brain masses are capable of awaking. And in the very highest animals, probably only monkeys and man, we find that the hemispheres have gone so far with their jealousy as to usurp the function of sensation. This is seen in the singular fact that with a monkey or man the removal of the cortical centres makes the animal permanently blind or deaf, as the case may be, while in the lower animals such removal does not have this result, so long as the "second-level" organs are unimpaired. The brain paths of the functions of the second and first levels taken together constitute the so-called "voluntary circuit" (see Fig. 2).

In addition to this general demarcation of functions as higher and lower--first, second, and third level--in their anatomical seat, many interesting discoveries have been made in the localization of the simpler functions in the cortex itself. The accompanying figures (Figs. 3 and 4) will show the principle centres which have been determined; and it is not necessary to dwell upon additional details which are still under discussion. The areas marked out are in general the same on both hemispheres, and that is to say that most of the centres are duplicated. The speech centres, however, are on one side only. And in certain cases the nervous fibres which connect the cortex with the body-organs cross below the brain to the opposite side of the body. This is always true in cases of muscular movement; the movements of the right side of the body are controlled by the left hemisphere, and vice versa. The stimulations coming in from the body to the brain generally travel on the same side, although in certain cases parallel impulses are also sent over to the other hemisphere as well. For example, the very important optic nerve, which is necessary to vision, comes from each eye separately in a large bunch of fibres, and divides at the base of the brain, so that each eye sends impulses directly to the visual centres of both hemispheres.

[Illustration: FIG. 3.--Outer surface of left hemisphere of the brain (modified from Exner): a, fissure of Rolando; b, fissure of Sylvius.]

[Illustration: FIG. 4.--Inner (mesial) surface of the right hemisphere of the brain (modified from Sch 鈜 er and Horsley). In both figures the shaded area is the motor zone.]

Of all the special questions which have arisen about the localization of functions in the nervous system, that of the function of certain areas known as "motor centres" has been eagerly discussed. The region on both sides of the fissure of Rolando in Fig. 3 contains a number of areas which give, when stimulated with electricity, very definite and regular movements of certain muscles on the opposite side of the body. By careful exploration of these areas the principal muscular combinations--those for facial movements, neck movements, movements of the arm, trunk, legs, tail, etc.--have been very precisely ascertained. It was concluded from these facts that these areas were respectively the centres for the discharge of the nervous impulses running in each case to the muscles which were moved. The evidence recently forthcoming, however, is leading investigators to think that there is no cortical centre for the "motor" or outgoing processes properly so called, and that these Rolandic areas, although called "motor," are really centres for the incoming reports of the movements of the respective muscles after the movements take place, and also for the preservation of the memories of movement which the mind must have before a particular movement can be brought about (the mental images of movement which we called on an earlier page Kinaesthetic Equivalents). These centres being aroused in the thought of the movement desired, which is the necessary mental preparation for the movement, they in turn stimulate the real motor centres which lie below the cortex at the second level. This is in the present writer's judgment the preferable interpretation of the evidence which we now have.

The Speech Zone.--Many interesting facts of the relation of body and mind have come to light in connection with the speech functions. Speech is complex, both on the psychological and also on the physiological side, and easily deranged in ways that take on such remarkable variety that they are a source of very fruitful indications to the inquirer. It is now proved that speech is not a faculty, a single definite capacity which a man either has or has not. It is rather a complex thing resulting from the combined action of many brain centres, and, on the mental side, of many so-called faculties, or functions. In order to speak a man normally requires what is called a "zone" in his brain, occupying a large portion of the outside lateral region (see Fig. 5). It extends, as in the figure, from the Rolandic region (K), where the kinaesthetic lip-and-tongue memories of words are aroused, backward into the temporal region (A), where the auditory memories of words spring up; then upward to the angular gyrus in the rear or occipital region (V), where in turn the visual pictures of the written or printed words rise to perform their part in the performance; and with all this combination there is associated the centre for the movements of the hand and arm employed in writing, an area higher up in the Rolandic region (above K). In the same general zone we also find the music function located, the musical sounds being received in the auditory centre very near the area for words heard (A) while the centre for musical expression is also in the Rolandic region. Furthermore, as may be surmised, the reading of musical notation requires the visual centre, just as does the reading of words. In addition to this, we find the curious fact that the location of the whole speech zone is in one hemisphere only. Its location on the left or the right, in particular cases, is also an indication as to whether the person is right-or left-handed; this means that the process which makes the individual either right or left-handed is probably located in the speech zone, or near it. A large majority of persons have the speech zone in the left hemisphere, and are right-handed; it will be seen that the figure (5) shows the left hemisphere of the brain, and with it the right hand holding the pen.

Defects of Speech--Aphasia.--The sorts of injury which may befall a large zone of the brain are so many that well-nigh endless forms of speech defect occur. All impairment of speech is called Aphasia, and it is called Motor Aphasia when the apparatus is damaged on the side of movement.

If the fibres coming out from the speech zone be impaired, so that the impulses can not go to the muscles of articulation and breathing, we have Subcortical Motor Aphasia. Its peculiarity is that the person knows perfectly what he wants to say, but yet can not speak the words. He is able to read silently, can understand the speech of others, and can remember music; but, with his inability to speak, he is generally also unable to write or to perform on a musical instrument (yet this last is not always the case). Then we find new variations if his "lesion"--as all kinds of local nervous defects are called-- is in the brain centre in the Rolandic region, where arise the memories of the movements required. In this latter case the aphasic patient can readily imitate speech so long as he hears it, can imitate writing so long as it lies before him, but can not do any independent speaking or writing for himself. With this there goes another fact which characterizes this form of aphasia, and which is called Cortical, as opposed to the Subcortical Motor Aphasia described above, that the person may not be able even to think of the words which are appropriate to express his meaning. This is the case when those persons who depend upon the memories of the movements of lip and tongue in their normal speech are injured as described.

Besides the two forms of Motor Aphasia now spoken of, there are certain other speech defects which are called Sensory Aphasia. When a lesion occurs in one of the areas of the brain in the speech zone in which the requisite memories of words seen or heard have their seat--as when a ball player is struck over the sight centre in the back of the head--special forms of sensory aphasia show themselves. The ball player will, in this case, have Visual Aphasia, being unable to speak in proportion as he is accustomed in his speaking to depend upon the images of written or printed words. He is quite unable to read or write from a copy which he sees; but he may be able, nevertheless, to write from dictation, and also to repeat words which are spoken to him. This is because in these latter performances he uses his auditory centre, and not the visual. There are, indeed, some persons who are so independent of vision that the loss of the visual centre does not much impair their normal speech.

When, again, an injury comes to the auditory centre in the temporal region, we find the converse of the case just described; the defect is then called Auditory Aphasia. The patient can not now speak or write words which he hears, and can not speak spontaneously in proportion as he is accustomed to depend upon his memories of the word sounds. But in most cases he can still both speak and write printed or written words which he sees before him.

These cases may serve to give the reader an idea of the remarkable delicacy and complexity of the function of speech. It becomes more evident when, instead of cases of gross lesion, which destroy a whole centre, or cut the connections between centres, we have disease of the brain which merely destroys a few cells in the gray matter here or there. We then find partial loss of speech, such as is seen in patients who lack only certain classes of words;

perhaps the verbs, or the conjunctions, or proper names, etc.; or in the patients who speak, but yet do not say what they mean; or, again, in persons who have two verbal series going on at once, one of which they can not control, and which they often attribute to an enemy inside them, in control of the vocal organs, or to a persecutor outside whose abuse they can not avoid hearing. In cases of violent sick headache we often miscall objects without detecting it ourselves, and in delirium the speech mechanism works from violent organic discharges altogether without control. The senile old man talks nonsense--so-called gibberish--thinking he is discoursing properly.

In the main cases of Aphasia of distinct sensory and motor types psychological analysis is now so adequate and the anatomical localization so far advanced that the physicians have sufficient basis for their diagnosis, and make inferences looking toward treatment. Many cases of tumour, of clot on the brain, of local pressure from the skull, and of h鎚 orrhage or stopping up of the blood vessels in a limited area, have been cured through the indications given by the particular forms and degrees of aphasia shown by the patients. The skull is opened at the place indicated by the defect of speech, the lesion found where the diagnosis suggested, and the cause removed.

This account of Localization will suggest to the reader the truth that there is no science of Phrenology. No progress has been made in localizing the intelligence; and the view is now very general that the whole brain, with all its interchange of impulses from part to part, is involved in thinking. As for locating particular emotions and qualities of temperament, it is quite absurd. Furthermore, the irregularities of the skull do not indicate local brain differences. It is thought that the relative weight of the brain may be an indication of intellectual endowment, especially when the brain weight is compared with the weight of the rest of the body, and that culture in particular lines increases the surface of the cortex by deepening and multiplying the convolutions. But these statements can not be applied off-hand to individuals, as the practise of phrenology would require.

Defects of Memory--Amnesia.--The cases given just above, where the failure of speech was seen to be due to the loss of certain memories of words, illustrate also a series of mental defects, which are classed together as Amnesias. Any failure in memory, except the normal lapses which we call forgetfulness, is included under this term. Just as the loss of word memories occasions inability to speak, so that of other sorts of memories occasions other functional disturbances. A patient may forget objects, and so not know how to use his penknife or to put on his shoes. He may forget events, and so give false witness as to the past.

One may forget himself also, and so have, in some degree, a different character, as is seen, in an exaggerated way, in persons who have so-called Dual Personality. These patients suddenly fall into a secondary state, in which they forget all the events of their ordinary lives, but remember all the events of the earlier periods of the secondary personality. This state may be described as "general" amnesia, in contrast to the "partial" amnesia of the other cases given, in which only particular classes of memories are impaired.

The impairment of memory with advancing years also illustrates both "general" and "partial" Amnesia. The old man loses his memory of names, then of other words, then of events, and so gradually becomes incapable of much retention of any sort.

Defects of Will--Aboulia.--A few words may suffice to characterize the great class of mental defects which arise on the side of action. All inability to perform intentional acts is called Aboulia, or lack of Will. Certain defects of speech mentioned above illustrate this: cases in which the patient knows what he wishes to say and yet can not say it. This is the type of all the "partial" Aboulias. There may be no lack in determination and effort, yet the action may be impossible. But, in contrast with this, there is a more grave defect called "general" Aboulia. Here we find a weakening of resolution, of determination, associated with some lack of self-control showing itself frequently by a certain hesitation or indecision. The patient says: "I can not make up my mind," "I can not decide." In exaggerated cases it becomes a form of mania called "insanity of doubt." The patient stands before a door for an hour hesitating as to whether he can open it or not, or carries to its extreme the experience we all sometimes have of finding it necessary to return again and again to make sure that we have locked the door or shut the draught of the furnace.

With these illustrations our notice of mental defects may terminate. The more complex troubles, the various insanities, manias, phobias, etc., can not be briefly described. Moreover, they are still wrapped in the profoundest obscurity. To the psychologist, however, there are certain guiding principles through the maze of facts, and I may state them in conclusion.

First, all mental troubles involve diseases of the brain and can be cured only as the brain is cured. It does not follow, of course, that in certain cases treatment by mental agencies, such as suggestion, arousing of expectation, faith, etc., may not be more helpful here, when wisely employed, than in troubles which do not involve the mind; but yet the end to be attained is a physical as well as a mental cure, and the means in the present state of knowledge, at any rate, are mainly physical means. The psychologist knows practically nothing about the laws which govern the influence of mind on body. The principle of Suggestion is so obscure in its concrete working that the most practised and best-informed operators find it impossible to control its use or to predict its results. To give countenance, in this state of things, to any pretended system or practice of mind cure, Christian science, spiritual healing, etc., which leads to the neglect of ordinary medical treatment, is to discredit the legitimate practice of medicine and to let loose an enemy dangerous to the public health.

Moreover, such things produce a form of hysterical subjectivism which destroys sound judgment, and dissolves the sense of reality which it has taken modern science many generations to build up. Science has all along had to combat such wresting of its more obscure and unexplained facts into alliance with the ends of practical quackery, fraud, and superstition; and psychologists need just now to be especially alive to their duty of combating the forms of this alliance which arise when the newer results of psychology are so used, whether it be to supplement the inadequate evidence of "thought-transference," to support the claims of spiritualism, or to justify in the name of "personal liberty" the substitution of a "healer" for the trained physician. The parent who allows his child to die under the care of a "Christian Science healer" is as much a criminal from neglect as the one who, going but a step further in precisely the same direction, brings his child to starvation on a diet of faith. In France and Russia experimenting in hypnotism on well persons has been restricted by law to licensed experts; what, compared with that, shall we say to this wholly amateurish experimenting with the diseased? Let the "healer" heal all he can, but let him not experiment to the extremity of life and death with the credulity and superstition of the people who think one "doctor" is as good as another.

Second, many experts agree that diseases of the mind, whatever their brain seat may be, all involve impairment of the Attention. This, at any rate, is a general mark of a deranged or defective mind. The idiot lacks power of attention. The maniac lacks control of his attention. The deluded lacks grasp and flexibility of attention. The crank can only attend to one thing. The old man is feeble in the attention, having lost his hold. So it goes. The attention is the instrument of the one sort of normal mental activity called Apperception, and so impairment of the attention shows itself at once in some particular form of defect.

Third, it is interesting to know that in progressive mental failure the loss of the powers of the mind takes place in an order which is the reverse of that of their original acquisition. The most complex functions, which are acquired last, are the first to show impairment. In cases of general degeneration, softening of the brain, etc., the intelligence and moral nature are first affected, then memory, association, and acquired actions of all sorts, while there remain, latest of all, actions of the imitative kind, most of the deep-set habits, and the instinctive, reflex, and automatic functions, This last condition is seen in the wretched victim of dementia and in the congenital idiot. The latter has, in addition to his life processes and instincts, little more than the capacity for parrot-like imitation. By this he acquires the very few items of his education.

The recovery of the patient shows the same stages again, but in the reversed direction; he pursues the order of the original acquisition, a process which physicians call Re-evolution.

CHAPTER VI.

HOW WE EXPERIMENT ON THE MIND--EXPERIMENTAL PSYCHOLOGY.

In recent years the growth of the method of experimenting with bodies in laboratories in the different sciences has served to raise the question whether the mind may not be experimented with also. This question has been solved in so far that psychologists produce artificial changes in the stimulations to the senses and in the arrangements of the objects and conditions existing about a person, and so secure changes also in his mental states. What we have seen of Physiological Psychology illustrates this general way of proceeding, for in such studies, changes in the physiological processes, as in breathing, etc., are considered as causing changes in the mind. In Experimental Psychology, however, as distinguished from Physiological Psychology, we agree to take only those influences which are outside the body, such as light, sound, temperature, etc., keeping the subject as normal as possible in all respects.

A great many laboratories have now been established in connection with the universities in Germany, France, and the United States. They differ very much from one another, but their common purpose is so to experiment upon the mind, through changes in the stimulations to which the individual is subjected, that tests may be made of his sensations, his ability to remember, the exactness and kind of movements, etc.

The working of these laboratories and the sort of research carried out in them may be illustrated best, perhaps, by a description of some of the results, apparatus, methods, etc., employed in my own laboratory during the past year. The end in view will, I trust, be considered sufficient justification for the degree of personal reference which this occasions; since greater concreteness and reality attach to definite descriptions such as this. The other laboratories, as those at Harvard and Columbia Universities, take up similar problems by similar methods. I shall therefore go on to describe some recent work in the Princeton laboratory.

Of the problems taken up in the laboratory, certain ones may be selected for somewhat detailed explanation, since they are from widely different spheres and illustrate different methods of procedure.

I. Experiments on the Temperature Sense.--For a score of years it has been suspected that we have a distinct sense, with a nerve apparatus of its own, for the feeling of different temperatures on the skin. Certain investigators found that this was probably true; it is proved by the fact that certain drugs alter the sensibility of the skin to hot and cold stimulations.

Another advance was made when it was found that sensations of either hot or cold may be had from regions which are insensible at the same time to the other sort of stimulation, cold or hot. Certain minute points were discovered which report cold when touched with a cold point, but give no feeling from a hot object; while other points would respond only with a sensation from heat, never giving cold. It was concluded that we have two temperature senses, one for hot and the other for cold.

Taking the problem at this point, Mr. C.[3] wished to define more closely the relation of the two sorts of sensation to each other, and thought he could do so by a method by which he might repeat the stimulation of a series of exact spots, very minute points on the skin, over and over again, thus securing a number of records of the results for both hot and cold over a given area. He chose an area of skin on the forearm, shaved it carefully, and proceeded to explore it with the smallest points of metals which could be drawn along the skin without pricking or tearing. These points were attached to metallic cylinders, and around the cylinders rubber bands were placed; the cylinders were then thrust in hot or cold water kept at certain regular temperatures, and lifted by the rubber bands. They were placed point down, with equal pressure, upon the points of the skin in the area chosen. In this way, points which responded only to hot, and also those responding only to cold, were found, marked with delicate ink marks in each case, until the whole area was explored and marked in different colours. This had often been done before. It remained to devise a way of keeping these records, so that the markings might all be removed from the skin, and new explorations made over the same surface. This was necessary in order to see whether the results secured were always the same. The theory that there were certain nervous endings in the skin corresponding to the little points required that each spot should be in exactly the same place whenever the experiment was repeated.

[Footnote 3: Mr. J. F. Crawford, graduate student.]

Mr. C. made a number of so-called "transparent transfer frames." They are rectangular pieces of cardboard, with windows cut in them. The windows are covered with thin architect's paper, which is very transparent. This frame is put over the forearm in such a way that the paper in the window comes over the markings made on the arm. The markings show through very clearly, and the points are copied on the paper. Then certain boundary marks at the corners are made, both on the paper and on the arm, at exactly the same places, the frame is removed, and all the markings on the arm are erased except the boundary points. The result is that at any time the frames can be put over the arm again by matching the boundary points, and then the original temperature spots on the skin will be shown by the markings on the paper window.

Proceeding to repeat the exploration of the same area in this way, Mr. C makes records of many groupings of points for both hot and cold sensations on the same area; he then puts the frames one upon another, holds them up before a window so that they have a bright background, and is thus able to see at a glance how nearly the results of the different sittings correspond.

His results, put very briefly, fail to confirm the theory that the sense of temperature has an apparatus of fixed spots for heat and other fixed spots for cold. For when he puts the different markings for heat together he finds that the spots are not the same, but that those of one frame fall between those of another, and if several are put together the points fill up a greater or smaller area. The same for the cold spots; they fill a continuous area. He finds, however, as other investigators have found, that the heat areas are generally in large measure separate from the cold areas, only to a certain extent overlapping here and there, and also that there are regions of the skin where we have very little sense of either sort of temperature.

The general results will show, therefore, if they should be confirmed by other investigators, that our temperature sense is located in what might be called somewhat large blotches on the skin, and not in minute spots; while the evidence still remains good, however, to show that we have two senses for temperature, one for cold and the other for hot.

II. Reaction-Time Experiments.--Work in so-called "reaction times" constitutes one of the most important and well-developed chapters in experimental psychology. In brief, the experiment involved is this: To find how long it takes a person to receive a sense impression of any kind--for example, to hear a sound-signal--and to move his hand or other member in response to the impression. A simple arrangement is as follows: Sit the subject comfortably, tap a bell in such a way that the tapping also makes an electric current and starts a clock, and instruct the subject to press a button with his finger as soon as possible after he hears the bell. The pressing of the button by him breaks the current and stops the clock. The dial of the clock indicates the actual time which has elapsed between the bell (signal) and his response with his finger (reaction). The clock used for exact work is likely to be the Hipp chronoscope, which gives on its dials indications of time intervals in thousandths of a second. For the sake of keeping the conditions constant and preventing disturbance, the wires are made long, so that the clock and the experimenter may be in one room, while the bell, the punch key, and the subject are in another, with the door closed. This method of getting reaction times has been in use for a number of years, especially by the astronomers who need to know, in making their observations, how much time is taken by the observer in recording a transit or other observation. It is part of the astronomer's "personal equation."

Proceeding with this "simple-reaction" experiment as a basis, the psychologists have varied the instructions to the subject so as to secure from him the different times which he takes for more complicated mental processes, such as distinguishing between two or more impressions, counting, multiplying, dividing, etc., before reacting; or they have him wait for an associated idea to come up before giving his response, with many other variations. By comparing these different times among themselves, interesting results are reached concerning the mental processes involved and also about the differences of different individuals in the simpler operations of their daily lives. The following research carried out by Mr. B.[4] serves to illustrate both of these assertions.

[Footnote 4: The writer.]

Mr. B. wished to inquire further into a fact found out by several persons by this method: the fact that there is an important difference in the length of a person's reaction time according to the direction of his attention during the experiment. If, for example, Mr. X. be tested, it is possible that he may prefer to attend strictly to the signal, letting his finger push the key without direct care and supervision. If this be true, and we then interfere with his way of proceeding, by telling him that he must attend to his finger, and allow the signal to take care of itself, we find that he has great difficulty in doing so, grows embarrassed, and his reaction time becomes very irregular and much longer. Yet another person, say Y, may show just the opposite state of things; he finds it easier to pay attention to his hand, and when he does so he gets shorter and also more regular times than when he attends to the signal-sound.

It occurred to Mr. B. that the striking differences given by different persons in this matter of the most favourable direction of the attention might be connected with the facts brought out by the physiological psychologists in connection with speech; namely, that one person is a "visual," in speaking, using mainly sight images of words, while another is a "motor," using mainly muscular images, and yet another an "auditive," using mainly sound images. If the differences are so marked in the matter of speech, it seemed likely that they might also extend to other functions, and the so-called "type" of a person in his speech might show itself in the relative lengths of his reaction times according as he attended to one class of images or another.

Calling this the "type theory" of reaction times, and setting about testing four different persons in the laboratory, the problem was divided into two parts; first, to direct all the individuals selected to find out, by examining their mental preferences in speaking, reading, writing, dreaming, etc., the class of images which they ordinarily depended most upon; and then to see by a series of experiments whether their reaction times to these particular classes of images were shorter than to others, and especially whether the times were shorter when attention was given to these images than when it was given to the muscles used in the reactions. The meaning of this would be that if the reaction should be shorter to these images than to the corresponding muscle images, or to the other classes of images, then the reaction time of an individual would show his mental type and be of use in testing it. This would be a very important matter if it should hold, seeing that many questions both in medicine and in education, which involve the ascertaining of the mental character of the individual person, would profit by such an exact method.

The results on all the subjects confirmed the supposition. For example, one of them, Mr. C., found from an independent examination of himself, most carefully made, that he depended very largely upon his hearing in all the functions mentioned. When he thought of words, he remembered how they sounded; when he dreamed, his dreams were full of conversation and other sounds. When he wrote, he thought continually of the way the words and sentences would sound if spoken. Without knowing of this, many series of reaction experiments were made on him; the result showed a remarkable difference between the lengths of his reactions, according as he directed his attention to the sound or to his hand; a difference showing his time to be one half shorter when he paid attention to the sound. The same was seen when he reacted to lights; the attention went preferably to the light, not to the hand; but the difference was less than in the case of sounds. So it was an unmistakable fact in his case that the results of the reaction experiments agreed with his independent decision as to his mental type.

In none of the cases did this correspondence fail, although all were not so pronounced in their type preferences as was Mr. C.

The second part of the research had in view the question whether reaction times taken upon speech would show the same thing; that is, whether in Mr. C.'s case, for example, it would be found that his reaction made by speaking, as soon as he heard the signal or saw the light, would be shorter when he paid attention to the signal than when he gave attention to his mouth and lips. For this purpose a mouth key was used which made it possible for the subject simply by emitting a puff of breath from the lips, to break an electric current and thus stop the chronoscope as soon as possible after hearing the signal. The mouth key is figured herewith (Fig. 6).

This experiment was also carried out on all the subjects, none of them having any knowledge of the end in view, and the experimenters also not having, as yet, worked out the results of the earlier research. In all the cases, again, the results showed that, for speech, the same thing held as for the hand--namely, that the shortest reaction times were secured when the subject paid attention to the class of images for which he had a general preference. In Mr. C.'s case, for example, it was found that the time it took him to speak was much shorter when he paid strict attention to the expected sound than when he attended to his vocal organs. So for the other cases. If the individual's general preference is for muscular images, we find that the quickest time is made when attention is given to the mouth and lips. Such is the case with Mr. B.

The general results go to show, therefore--and four cases showing no exception, added to the indications found by other writers, make a general conclusion very probable--that in the differences in reaction times, as secured by giving the attention this way or that, we have general indications of the individual's temperament, or at least of his mental preferences as set by his education. These indications agree with those found in the cases of aphasia known as "motor," "visual," "auditory," etc., already mentioned. The early examination of children by this method would probably be of great service in determining proper courses of treatment, subjects of study, modes of discipline, tendencies to fatigue and embarrassment, and the direction of best progress in education.

This research may be taken to illustrate the use of the reaction-time method in investigating such complex processes as attention, temperament, etc. The department which includes the various time measurements in psychology is now called Mental Chronometry, the older term, Psychometry, being less used on account of its ambiguity.

III. An Optical Illusion.--In the sphere of vision many very interesting facts are constantly coming to light. Sight is the most complex of the senses, the most easily deranged, and, withal, the most necessary to our normal existence. The report of the following experimental study will have the greater utility, since, apart from any intrinsic novelty or importance the results may prove to have, it shows some of the general bearings of the facts of vision in relation to 苊 thetics, to the theory of Illusions, and to the function of Judgment.

Illusion of the senses is due either to purely physiological causes or to the operation of the principle of Assimilation, which has already been remarked upon. In the latter case it illustrates the fact that at any time there is a general disposition of the mind to look upon a thing under certain forms, patterns, etc., to which it has grown accustomed; and to do this it is led sometimes to distort what it sees or hears unconsciously to itself. So it falls into errors of judgment through the trap which is set by its own manner of working. Nowhere is the matter better illustrated than in the sphere of vision. The number of illusions of vision is remarkable. We are constantly taking shapes and forms for something slightly different from what, by measurement, we actually find them to be. And psychologists are attempting--with rather poor success so far--to find some general principles of the mechanism of vision which will account for the great variety of its illusions.

Among these principles one is known as Contrast. It is hardly a principle as yet. It is rather a word used to cover all illusions which spring up when surfaces of different sizes and shapes, looked at together or successively, are misjudged with reference to one another. Wishing to investigate this in a simple way, the following experiment was planned and carried out by Mr. B.

He wished to find out whether, if two detached surfaces of different sizes be gazed at together, the linear distances of the field of vision (the whole scene visible at once) would be at all misjudged. To test this, he put in the window (W)[5] of the dark room a filling of white cardboard in which two square holes had been cut (S S'). The sides of the squares were of certain very unequal lengths. Then a slit was made between the middle points of the sides of the squares next to each other, so that there was a narrow path or trough joining the squares between their adjacent sides. Inside the dark room he arranged a bright light so that it would illuminate this trough, but not be seen by a person seated some distance in front of the window in the next room. A needle (D) was hung on a pivot behind the cardboard, so that its point could move along the bright trough in either direction; and on the needle was put the armature (A) of an electro-magnet which, when a current passed, would be drawn instantly to the magnet (E), and so stop the needle exactly at the point which it had then reached. A clock motor (Cm) was arranged in such a way as to carry the needle back and forth regularly over the slit; and the electro-magnet was connected by wires with a punch key (K) on a table beside the subject in the next room. All being now ready, the subject, Mr. S., is told to watch the needle which appears as a bead of light travelling along the slit, and stop it when it comes to the middle point of the line, by pressing the electric key. The experimenter, who stands behind the window in the dark room, reads on a scale (mm.) marked in millimetres the exact point at which the needle stops, releases the needle by breaking the current, thus allowing it to return slowly over the line again. This gives the subject another opportunity to stop it at what he judges to be the exact middle of the line, and so on. The accompanying figure (Fig. 7) shows the entire arrangement.

[Footnote 5: This and the following letters in parentheses refer to Fig. 7]

A great many experiments performed in this way, with the squares set both vertically and horizontally, and with several persons, brought a striking and very uniform result. The point selected by the subject as the middle is regularly too far toward the smaller square. Not a little, indeed, but a very appreciable amount. The amount of the displacement, or, roughly speaking, of the illusion, increases as the larger square is made larger and the smaller one smaller; or, put in a sentence, the amount varies directly with the ratio of the smaller to the larger square side.

Finding such an unmistakable illusion by this method, Mr. B. thought that if it could be tested by an appeal to people generally, it would be of great gain. It occurred to him that the way to do this would be to reverse the conditions of the experiment in the following way: He prepared the figures given in Plate I, in which the two squares are made of suitable relative size, a line is drawn between them, and a point on the line is plainly marked. This he had printed in a weekly journal, and asked the readers of the journal to get their friends, after merely looking at the figure (i. e., without knowing the result to be expected), to say--as the reader may now do before reading further--whether the point on the line (Plate I) is in the middle or not; and if not, in which direction from the true middle it lies. The results from hundreds of persons of all manner of occupations, ages, and of both sexes, agree in saying that the point lies too far toward the larger square. In reality it is in the exact middle. This is just the opposite of the result of the experiments in the laboratory, where the conditions were the reverse, i. e., to find the middle as it appears to the eye. Here, therefore, we have a complete confirmation of the illusion; and it is now fully established that in all cases in which the conditions of this experiment are realized we make a constant mistake in estimating distances by the eye.[6]

[Footnote 6: In redrawing the figure on a larger sheet (which is recommended), the connecting line may be omitted, only the mid-point being marked. Some get a better effect with two circles, the intervening distance being divided midway by a dot, as in Plate II.]

For instance, if a town committee wish to erect a statue to their local hero in the public square, and if on two opposite sides of the square there are buildings of very different heights, the statue should not be put in the exact middle of the square, if it is to give the best effect from a distance. It should be placed a little toward the smaller building. A colleague of the writer found, when this was first made public, that the pictures in his house had actually been hung in such a way as to allow for this illusion. Whenever a picture was to be put up between two others of considerable difference of size, or between a door (large) and a window (small), it had actually been hung a little nearer to the smaller--toward the small picture or toward the window-- and not in the true middle.

It is probable that interesting applications of this illusion may be discovered in aesthetics. For wherever in drawing or painting it is wished to indicate to the observer that a point is midway between two lines of different lengths, we should find that the artist, in order to produce this effect most adequately, deviates a little from the true middle. So in architecture, the effect of a contrast of masses often depends upon the sense of bilateral balance, symmetry, or equality, in which this visual error would naturally come into play. Indeed, it is only necessary to recall to mind that one of the principal laws of aesthetic effect in the matter of right line proportion is the relation of "one to one," as it is called, or equal division, to see the wide sphere of application of this illusion. In all such cases the mistake of judgment would have to be allowed for if masses of unequal size lie at the ends of the line which is to be divided.

IV. The Accuracy of Memory.--Another investigation may be cited to illustrate quite a different department. It aimed to find out something about the rate at which memory fades with the lapse of time. Messrs. W., S., and B.[7] began by formulating the different ways in which tests may be made on individuals to see how accurate their memories are after different periods of time. They found that three different tests might be employed, and called them "methods" of investigating memory. These are, first, the method of Reproduction. The individual is asked to reproduce, as in an oral or written examination, what he remembers of something told him a certain time before. This is the ordinary method of the schools and colleges, of civil-service examinations, etc. Second, the method of Identification, which calls upon the person to identify a thing, sentence, report, etc., a second or third time, as being the same in all respects as that which he experienced the first time it appeared. Third, the method of Selection, in which we show to the person a number of things, sentences, reports, descriptions of objects, etc., and require him to select from them the ones which are exactly the same as those he has had before. These methods will be better understood from the account now to be given of the way they were carried out on a large number of students.

[Footnote 7: Prof. H. C. Warren, Mr. W. J. Shaw, and the writer.]

The first experiments were made by Messrs. S. and B. in the University of

Toronto on a class of students numbering nearly three hundred, of whom about one third were women. The instructors showed to the class certain squares of cardboard of suitable size, and asked them to do the following three things on different days: First, to reproduce from memory, with pencil on paper, squares of the same size as those shown, after intervals of one, ten, twenty, and forty minutes (this gives results by the method of Reproduction); second, to say whether a new set of squares, which were shown to them after the same intervals, were the same in size as those which they had originally seen, smaller, or larger (illustrating the method of Identification); third, they were shown a number of squares of slightly different sizes, again at the same intervals, and asked to select from them the ones which they found to be the same size as those originally seen (method of Selection).

The results from all these experiments were combined with those of another series, secured from a large class of Princeton students; and the figure (Fig. 8) shows by curves something of the result. The figure is given in order that the reader may understand by its explanation the "graphic method" of plotting statistical results, which, with various complications, is now employed in psychology as well as in the other positive sciences.

[Illustration: FIG. 8.--Memory curves: I. Method of Selection. II. Method of Identification.]

Briefly described in words, it was found that the three methods agreed (the curves are parallel)[8] in showing that during the first ten minutes there was a great falling off in the accuracy of memory (slant in the curves from 0 to 10); that then, between ten and twenty minutes, memory remained relatively faithful (the curves are nearly level from 10 to 20), and that a rapid falling off in accuracy occurred after twenty minutes (shown by the slant in the lines from 20 to 40).

[Footnote 8: This figure shows curves for two of the methods only, Selection and Identification.]

Further, the different positions of the curves show certain things when properly understood. The curve secured by the method of Reproduction (not given in the figure) shows results which are least accurate, because most variable. The reason of this is that in drawing the squares to reproduce the one remembered, the student is influenced by the size of the paper he uses, by the varying accuracy of his control over his hand and arm (the results vary, for example, according as he uses his right or left hand), and by all sorts of associations with square objects which may at the time be in his mind. In short, this method gives his memory of the square a chance to be fully assimilated to his current mental state during the interval, and there is no corrective outside of him to keep him true.

That this difficulty is a real one no one who has examined students will be disposed to deny. When we ask them to reproduce what the text-book or the professor's lectures have taught, we also ask them to express themselves accurately. Now the science of correct expression is a thing in which the average student has had no training. With his difficulty in remembering is connected his difficulty of expression; and with it all goes a certain embarrassment, due to responsibility, personal fear, and dread of disgrace. So the results finally obtained by this method are really very complex.

One of the curves, that given by the method of Selection (I), also shows memory to be interfered with by a certain influence. We saw in connection with the experiments reported above that, even in the most elementary arrangements of squares in the visual fields, an element of contrast comes in to interfere with our judgment of size. This we find confirmed in these experiments when the method of Selection is used. By this method we show a number of squares side by side, asking the individual to select the one he saw before. All the squares, being shown at once, come into contrast with one another on the background; and so his judgment of the size of the one he remembers is distorted. This, again, is a real influence in our mental lives, leading to actual illusion. An unscrupulous lawyer may gradually modify the story which his client or a witness tells by constantly adding to what is really remembered, other details so expertly contrasted with the facts, or so neatly interposed among them, that the witness gradually incorporates them in his memory and so testifies more nearly as the lawyer desires. In our daily lives another element of contrast is also very strong--that due to social opinion. We constantly modify our memories to agree more closely with the truths of social belief, paring down unconsciously the difference between our own and others' reports of things. If several witnesses of an event be allowed to compare notes from time to time, they will gradually come to tell more nearly the same story.

The other curve (II) in the figure, that secured by the method of Identification, seemed to the investigators to be the most accurate. It is not subject to the errors due to expression and to contrast, and it has the advantage of allowing the subject the right to recognise the square. It is shown to him again, with no information that it is the same, and he decides whether from his remembrance of the earlier one, it is the same or not. The only objection to this method is that it requires a great many experiments in order to get an average result. To be reliable, an average must be secured, seeing that, for one or two or a few trials, the student may guess right without remembering the original square at all. By taking a large number of persons, such as the three hundred students, this objection may be overcome. Comparing the averages, for example, of the results given by the men and women respectively, we found practically no difference between them.

This last point may serve to introduce a distinction which is important in all work in experimental psychology, and one which is recognised also in many other sciences--the distinction between results obtained respectively from one individual and from many. Very often the only way to learn truth about a single individual is to investigate a number together. In all large classes of things, especially living things, there are great individual differences, and in any particular case this personal variation may be so large that it obscures the real nature of the normal. For example, three large sons may be born to two small parents; and from this case alone it might be inferred that all small parents have large sons. Or three girls might have better memories than three boys in the same family or school, and from this it might be argued that girls are better endowed in this direction than boys. In all such cases the proper thing to do is to get a large number of cases and combine them; then the preponderance which the first cases examined may have shown, in one direction or the other, is corrected. This gives rise to what is called the statistical method; it is used in many practical matters, such as life insurance, but its application to the facts of life, mind, variation, evolution, etc., is only begun. Its neglect in psychology is one of the crying defects of much recent work. Its use in complicated problems involves a mathematical training which people generally do not possess; and its misuse through lack of exactness of observation or ignorance of the requirements is worse than its neglect.

Another result came out in connection with these experiments on memory, which, apart from its practical interest, may serve to show an additional resource of experimental psychology. In making up the results of a series of experiments it is very important to observe the way in which the different cases differ from one another. Some cases may be so nearly alike that the most extreme of them are not far from the average of them all; as we find, for example, if we measure a thousand No. 10 shot. But now suppose we mix in with the No. 10 some No. 6 and some No. 14, and then take the average size; we may now get just the same average, and we can tell that this pile is different from the other only by observing the individual measurements of the single shot and setting down the relative frequency of each particular size. Or, again, we may get a different average size in one of two ways: either by taking another lot of uniform No. 14 shot, let us say, or by mixing with the No. 10 a few very large bullets. Which is actually the case would be shown only by the examination of the individual cases. This is usually done by comparing each case with the average of the whole lot, and taking the average of the differences thus secured--a quantity called the "mean variation."

In the case of the experiments with the squares, the errors in the judgments of the students were found to lie always in one direction. The answers all tended to show that they took, for the one originally shown, a square which was really too large. Casting about for the reason of this, it was considered necessary to explain it by the supposition that the square remembered had in the interval become enlarged in memory. The image was larger when called up after ten or twenty minutes than it was before. This might be due to a purely mental process; or possibly to a sort of spreading-out of the brain process in the visual centre, giving the result that whenever, by the revival of the brain process, the mental image is brought back again to mind, this spreading out shows itself by an enlargement of the memory image. However it may be explained, the indications of it were unmistakable--unless, of course, some other reason can be given for the uniform direction of the errors; and it is further seen in other experiments carried out by Messrs. W. and B. and by Dr. K.[9] at a later date.

[Footnote 9: Dr. F. Kennedy, demonstrator, now professor in the University of Colorado (results not yet published).]

If this tendency to the enlargement of our memories with the lapse of time should be found to be a general law of memory, it would have interesting bearings. It would suggest, for instance, an explanation of the familiar fact that the scenes of the past seem to us, when we return to them, altogether too small. Our childhood home, the old flower garden, the height of house and trees, and even that of our hero uncle, all seem to the returning traveller of adult life ridiculously small. That we expect them to be larger may result from the fact that the memory images have undergone change in the direction of enlargement.

V. Suggestion.--Space permits only the mention of another research, which, however, should not be altogether omitted, since it illustrates yet other problems and the principles of their solution. This is an investigation by Messrs. T. and H.,[10] which shows the remarkable influence of mental suggestions upon certain bodily processes which have always been considered purely physiological. These investigators set out to repeat certain experiments of others which showed that if two points, say those of a pair of compasses, be somewhat separated and put upon the skin, two sensations of contact come from the points. But if while the experiment is being performed the points be brought constantly nearer to each other, a time arrives when the two are felt as only one, although they may be still some distance apart. The physiologists argued from this that there were minute nerve endings in the skin at least so far apart as the least distance at which the points were felt as two; and that when the points were so close together that they only touched one of these nerve endings, only one sensation was produced. Mr. T. had already found, working in Germany, that, with practice, the skin gradually became more and more able to discriminate the two points--that is, to feel the two at smaller distances; and, further, that the exercise of the skin in this way on one side of the body not only made that locality more sensitive to minute differences, but had the same effect, singularly, on the corresponding place on the other side of the body. This, our experimenters inferred, could only be due to the continued suggestion in the mind of the subject that he should feel two points, the result being an actual heightening of the sensibility of the skin. When he thought that he was becoming more sensitive on one side--and really was--this sense or belief of his took effect in some way in both hemispheres of his brain, and so both sides of the body were alike affected.

[Footnote 10: G. A. Tawney, now professor in Beloit College, and C. W. Hodge, now professor in Lafayette College.]

This led to other experiments in Princeton in which suggestions were actually made to the subjects that they were to become more or less sensitive to distance and direction between the points on the skin, with the striking result that these suggestions actually took effect all over the body. This was so accurately determined that from the results of the experiments with the compasses on the skin in this case or that, pretty accurate inferences could be made as to what mental suggestions the subject was getting at the time. There was no chance for deception in the results, for the experiments were so controlled that the subject did not know until afterward of the correspondences actually reached between his states of mind and the variations in sensibility of the skin.

This slight report of the work done in one laboratory in about two sessions, involving a considerable variety of topics, may give an idea, so far as it goes, of the sort of work which experimental psychology is setting itself to do. It will be seen that there is as yet no well-knit body of results on which new experiments may proceed, and no developed set of experimental arrangements, such as other positive sciences show. The procedure is, in many important matters, still a matter of the individual worker's judgment and ability. Even for the demonstrations attempted for undergraduate students, good and cheap apparatus is still lacking. For these reasons it is premature as yet to expect that this branch of the science will cut much of a figure in education. There can be no doubt, however, that it is making many interesting contributions to our knowledge of the mind, and that when it is more adequately organized and developed in its methods and apparatus, It will become the basis of discipline of a certain kind lying between that of physical science and that of the humanities, since it will have features in common with the biological and natural sciences. Its results may be expected also to lead to better results than we now have in the theory and practice of education.

CHAPTER VII.

SUGGESTION IN CHILDREN AND ADULTS--HYPNOTISM.

In an earlier place certain illustrations of Suggestion have been given. By Suggestion we mean the fact that all sorts of hints from without disturb and modify the beliefs and actions of the individual. Certain cases from my own observation may be given which will make the matter clear.

Physiological Suggestion.--Observation of an infant for the first month or six weeks after birth leads to the conviction that his life is mainly physiological. When the actions which are purely reflex, together with certain random impulsive movements, are noted, we seem to exhaust the case.

Yet even at this remarkably early stage H. was found to be in some degree receptive to certain Suggestions conveyed by repeated stimulation under uniform conditions. In the first place, the suggestions of sleep began to tell upon her before the end of the first month. Her nurse put her to sleep by laying her face down and patting gently upon the end of her spine. This position soon became itself not only suggestive to the child of sleep, but sometimes necessary to sleep, even when she was laid across the nurse's lap in what seemed to be an uncomfortable position.

This case illustrates what may be called Physiological Suggestion. It shows the law of physiological habit as it borders on the conscious.

The same sort of phenomena appear also in adult life. Positions given to the limbs of a sleeper lead to movements ordinarily associated with these positions. The sleeper defends himself, withdraws himself from cold, etc. Children learn gradually to react upon conditions of position, lack of support, etc., of the body, with those actions necessary to keep from falling, which adults have so perfectly. All secondary automatic reactions may be classed here; the sensations coming from one action, as in walking, being suggestions to the next movement, unconsciously acted upon. The consciousness at any stage in the chain of movements, if present at all, must be similar to the baby's in the case above--a mere internal glimmering. The most we can say of such physiological suggestion is, that there is probably some consciousness, and that the ordinary reflexes seem to be abbreviated and improved.

Subconscious Adult Suggestion.--There are certain phenomena of a rather striking kind coming under this head whose classification is so evident that we may enumerate them without discussion of the general principles which they involve.

Tune Suggestion.--It has been pointed out recently that dream states are largely indebted for their visual elements--what we see in our dreams--to accidental lines, patches, etc., in the field of vision when the eyes are shut, due to the distended blood vessels of the cornea and lids, to changes in the external illumination, to the presence of dust particles of different configuration, etc. The other senses also undoubtedly contribute to the texture of our dreams by equally subconscious suggestions. There is no doubt, further, that our waking life is constantly influenced by such trivial stimulations.

I have tested in detail, for example, the conditions of the rise of so-called "internal tunes"--we speak of "tunes in our head" or "in our ears"--and find certain suggestive influences which in most cases cause these tunes to rise and take their course. Often, when a tune springs up "in my head," the same tune has been lately sung or whistled in my hearing, though quite unnoticed at the time. Often the tunes are those heard in church the previous day or earlier. Such a tune I am entirely unable to recall voluntarily; yet when it comes into the mind's ear, so to speak, I readily recognise it as belonging to an earlier day's experience. Other cases show various accidental suggestions, such as the tune Mozart suggested by the composer's name, the tune Gentle Annie suggested by the name Annie, etc. In all these cases it is only after the tune has taken possession of consciousness and after much seeking that the suggesting influence is discovered.

Closer analysis reveals certain additional facts: The "time" of such internal tunes is usually dictated by some rhythmical subconscious occurrence. After hearty meals it is always the time of the heart beat, unless there be "in the air" some more impressive stimulus; as, for example, when on shipboard, the beat is with me invariably that of the engine throbs. When walking it is the rhythm of the footfall. On one occasion a knock of four beats on the door started the Marseillaise in my ear; following up this clew, I found that at any time different divisions of musical time being struck on the table at will by another person, tunes would spring up and run on, getting their cue from the measures suggested. Further, when a tune dies away, its last notes often suggest, some time after, another having a similar movement--just as we pass from one tune to another in a "medley." It may also be noted that in my case the tune memories are auditive: they run in my head when I have no words for them and have never sung them--an experience which is consistent with the fact that these "internal tunes" arise in childhood before the faculty of speech. They also have distinct pitch. For example, I once found a tune "in my head" which was perfectly familiar, but for which I could find no words. Tested on the piano, the pitch was F-sharp and the time was my heart beat. Finally, after much effort, I got the unworthy words "Wait till the clouds roll by" by humming the tune over repeatedly. The pitch is determined probably by the accidental condition of the auditory centre in the brain or by the pitch of the external sound which serves as stimulus to the tune.

Normal Auto-Suggestion.--A further class of Suggestions, which fall under the general phrase Auto-suggestion, or Self-suggestion of a normal type, may be illustrated. In experimenting upon the possibility of suggesting sleep to another I have found certain strong reactive influences upon my own mental condition. Such an effort, which involves the picturing of another as asleep, is a strong Auto-suggestion of sleep, taking effect in my own case in about five minutes if the conditions be kept constant. The more clearly the patient's sleep is pictured the stronger becomes the subjective feeling of drowsiness. After about ten minutes the ability to give strong concentration seems to disintegrate, attention is renewed only by fits and starts and in the presence of great, mental inertia, and the oncoming of sleep is almost overpowering. An unfailing cure for insomnia, speaking for myself, is the persistent effort to put some one else asleep by hard thinking of the end in view, with a continued gentle movement, such as stroking the other with the hand.

On the other hand, it is impossible to bring on a state of drowsiness by imagining myself asleep. The first effort at this, indeed, is promising, for it leads to a state of restfulness and ease akin to the mental composure which is the usual preliminary to sleep; but it goes no further. It is succeeded by a state of steady wakefulness, which effort of attention or effort not to attend only intensifies. If the victim of insomnia could only forget that he is thus afflicted, could forget himself altogether, his case would be more hopeful. The contrast between this condition and that already described shows that it is the Self-idea, with the emotions it awakens,[11] which prevents the suggestion from realizing itself and probably accounts for many cases of insomnia.

[Footnote 11: A friend informs me that when he pictures himself dead he can not help feeling gratified that he makes so handsome a corpse.]

Sense Exaltation.--Recent discussions of Hypnotism have shown the remarkable "exaltation" which the senses may attain in somnambulism, together with a corresponding refinement in the interpretative faculty. This is described more fully below. Events, etc., quite subconscious, usually become suggestions of direct influence upon the subject. Unintended gestures, habitual with the experimenter, may suffice to hypnotize his accustomed subject. The possibility of such training of the senses in the normal state has not had sufficient emphasis. The young child's subtle discriminations of facial and other personal indications are remarkable. The prolonged experience of putting H. to sleep--extending over a period of more than six months, during which I slept beside her bed--served to make me alive to a certain class of suggestions otherwise quite beyond notice. It is well known that mothers are awake to the needs of their infants when they are asleep to everything else.

In the first place, we may note the intense auto-suggestion of sleep already pointed out, under the stimulus of repeated nursery rhymes or other regular devices regularly resorted to in putting the child asleep. Second, surprising progressive exaltation of the hearing and interpretation of sounds coming from her in a dark room. At the end of four or five months, her movements in bed awoke me or not according as she herself was awake or not. Frequently after awaking I was distinctly aware of what movements of hers had awaked me.[12] A movement of her head by which it was held up from the pillow was readily distinguished from the restless movements of her sleep. It was not so much, therefore, exaltation of hearing as exaltation of the function of the recognition of sounds heard and of their discrimination.

[Footnote 12: This fact is analogous to our common experience of being awaked by a loud noise and then hearing it after we awake; yet the explanation is not the same.]

Again, the same phenomenon to an equally marked degree attended the sound of her breathing. It is well enough known that the smallest functional bodily changes induce changes in both the rapidity and the quality of the respiration. In sleep the muscles of inhalation and exhalation are relaxed, inhalation becomes long and deep, exhalation short and exhaustive, and the rhythmic intervals of respiration much lengthened. Now degrees of relative wakefulness are indicated with surprising delicacy by the slight respiration sounds given forth by the sleeper. Professional nurses learn to interpret these indications with great skill. This exaltation of hearing became very pronounced in my operations with the child. After some experience the peculiar breathing of advancing or actual wakefulness in her was sufficient to wake me. And when awake myself the change in the infant's respiration sounds to those indicative of oncoming sleep was sufficient to suggest or bring on sleep in myself. In the dark, also, the general character of her breathing sounds was interpreted with great accuracy in terms of her varied needs, her comfort or discomfort, etc. The same kind of suggestion from the respiration sounds now troubles me whenever one of the children is sleeping within hearing distance.[13]

[Footnote 13: This is an unpleasant result which is confirmed by professional infants' nurses. They complain of loss of sleep when off duty. Mrs. James Murray, an infants' nurse in Toronto, informs me that she finds it impossible to sleep when she has no infant in hearing distance, and for that reason she never asks for a vacation. Her normal sleep has evidently come to depend upon continuous soporific suggestions from a child. In another point, also, her experience confirms my observations, viz., the child's movements, preliminary to waking, awake her, when no other movements of the child do so--the consequence being that she is ready for the infant when it gets fully awake and cries out.]

The reactions in movement upon these suggestions are very marked and appropriate, in customary or habitual lines, although the stimulations are quite subconscious. The clearest illustrations in this body of my experiences were afforded by my responses in crude songs to the infant's waking movements and breathing sounds. I have often waked myself by myself singing one of two nursery rhymes, which by endless repetition night after night had become so habitual as to follow in an automatic way upon the stimulus from the child. It is certainly astonishing that among the things which one may get to do automatically, we should find singing; but writers on the subject have claimed that the function of musical or semi-musical expression may be reflex.

The principle of subconscious suggestion, of which these simple facts are less important illustrations, has very interesting applications in the higher reaches of social, moral, and educational theory.

Inhibitory Suggestion.--An interesting class of phenomena which figure perhaps at all the levels of nervous action now described, may be known as Inhibitory Suggestions. The phrase, in its broadest use, refers to all cases in which the suggesting stimulus tends to suppress, check, or inhibit movement. We find this in certain cases just as strongly marked as the positive movement--bringing kind of suggestion. The facts may be put under certain heads which follow.

Pain Suggestion.--Of course, the fact that pain inhibits movement occurs at once to the reader. So far as this is general, and is a native inherited thing, it is organic, and so falls under the head of Physiological Suggestion of a negative sort. The child shows contracting movements, crying movements, starting and jumping movements, shortly after birth, and so plainly that we need not hesitate to say that these pain responses belong purely to his nervous system; and that, in general, they are inhibitory and contrary to those other native reactions which indicate pleasure.

The influence of pain extends everywhere through mental development, however. Its general effect is to dampen down or suppress the function which brings the pain; and in this its action is just the contrary to that of pleasure, which furthers the pleasurable function.

Control Suggestion.--This covers all cases which show any kind of restraint set upon the movements of the body short of that which comes from voluntary intention. The infant brings the movements of his legs, arms, head, etc., gradually into some sort of order and system. It is accomplished by a system of organic checks and counter-checks, by which associations are formed between muscular sensations on the one hand and certain other sensations, as of sight, touch, hearing, etc., on the other hand. The latter serve as suggestions to the performance of these movements, and these alone. The infant learns to balance his head and trunk, to direct his hands, to grasp with thumb opposite the four fingers--all largely by such control suggestions, aided, of course, by his native reflexes.

Contrary Suggestion.--By this is meant a tendency of a very striking kind observable in many children, no less than in many adults, to do the contrary when any course is suggested. The very word "contrary" is used in popular talk to describe an individual who shows this type of conduct. Such a child or man is rebellious whenever rebellion is possible; he seems to kick constitutionally against the pricks.

The fact of "contrariness" in older children--especially boys--is so familiar to all who have observed school children with any care that I need not cite further details. And men and women often become so enslaved to suggestions of the contrary that they seem only to wait for indications of the wishes of others in order to oppose and thwart them.

Contrary suggestions are to be explained as exaggerated instances of control. It is easy to see that the checks and counter-checks already spoken of as constituting the method of control of muscular movement may themselves become so habitual and intense as to dominate the reactions which they should only regulate. The associations between the muscular series and the visual series, let us say, which controls it, comes to work backward, so that the drift of the organic processes is toward certain contrary reverse movements.

In the higher reaches of conduct and life we find interesting cases of very refined contrary suggestion. In the man of ascetic temperament, the duty of self-denial takes the form of a regular contrary suggestion in opposition to every invitation to self-indulgence, however innocent. The over-scrupulous mind, like the over-precise, is a prey to the eternal remonstrances from the contrary which intrude their advice into all his decisions. In matters of thought and belief also cases are common of stubborn opposition to evidence, and persistence in opinion, which are in no way due to the cogency of the contrary arguments or to real force of conviction.

Hypnotic Suggestion.--The facts upon which the current theories of hypnotism are based may be summed up under a few headings, and the recital of them will serve to bring this class of phenomena into the general lines of classification drawn out in this chapter.

The Facts.--When by any cause the attention is held fixed upon an object, say a bright button, for a sufficient time without distraction, the subject begins to lose consciousness in a peculiar way. Generalizing this simple experiment, we may say that any method or device which serves to secure undivided and prolonged attention to any sort of Suggestion--be it object, idea, anything that is clear and striking--brings on what is called Hypnosis to a person normally constituted.

The Paris school of interpreters find three stages of progress in the hypnotic sleep: First, Catalepsy, characterized by rigid fixity of the muscles in any position in which the limbs may be put by the experimenter, with great Suggestibility on the side of consciousness, and An鑑thesia (lack of sensation) in certain areas of the skin and in certain of the special senses; second, Lethargy, in which consciousness seems to disappear entirely; the subject not being sensitive to any stimulations by eye, ear, skin, etc., and the body being flabby and pliable as in natural sleep; third, Somnambulism, so called from its analogies to the ordinary sleep-walking condition to which many persons are subject. This last covers the phenomena of ordinary mesmeric exhibitions at which travelling mesmerists "control" persons before audiences and make them obey their commands. While other scientists properly deny that these three stages are really distinct, they may yet be taken as representing extreme instances of the phenomena, and serve as points of departure for further description.

On the mental side the general characteristics of hypnotic Somnambulism are as follows:

1. The impairment of memory in a peculiar way. In the hypnotic condition all affairs of the ordinary life are forgotten; on the other hand, after waking the events of the hypnotic condition are forgotten. Further, in any subsequent period of Hypnosis the events of the former similar periods are remembered. So a person who is frequently hypnotized has two continuous memories: one for the events of his normal life, exercised only when he is normal; and one for the events of his hypnotic periods, exercised only when he is hypnotized.

2. Suggestibility to a remarkable degree. By this is meant the tendency of the subject to have in reality any mental condition which is suggested to him. He is subject to Suggestions both on the side of his sensations and ideas and also on the side of his actions. He will see, hear, remember, believe, refuse to see, hear, etc., anything, with some doubtful exceptions, which may be suggested to him by word or deed, or even by the slightest and perhaps unconscious indications of those about him. On the side of conduct his

suggestibility is equally remarkable. Not only will he act in harmony with the illusions of sight, etc., into which he is led, but he will carry out, like an automaton, the actions suggested to him. Further, pain and pleasure, with their organic accompaniments may be produced by Suggestion. The skin may be actually scarred with a lead pencil if the patient be told that it is red-hot iron. The suggested pain brings about vasomotor and other bodily changes that prove, as similar tests in the other cases prove, that simulation is impossible and the phenomena are real. These truths and those given below are no longer based on the mere reports of the "mesmerists," but are the recognised property of legitimate psychology.

Again, such suggestions may be for a future time, and be performed only when a suggested interval has elapsed; they are then called Deferred or Post-hypnotic Suggestions. Post-hypnotic Suggestions are those which include the command not to perform them until a certain time after the subject has returned to his normal condition; such suggestions--if of reasonably trifling character--are actually carried out afterward in the normal state, although the person is conscious of no reason why he should act in such a way, having no remembrance whatever that he has received the suggestion when hypnotized. Such post-hypnotic performances may be deferred by suggestion for many months.

3. So-called Exaltation of the mental faculties, especially of the senses: increased acuteness of vision, hearing, touch, memory, and the mental functions generally. By reason of this great "exaltation," hypnotized patients may get suggestions from the experimenters which are not intended, and discover their intentions when every effort is made to conceal them. Often emotional changes in expression are discerned by them; and if it be admitted that their power of logical and imaginative insight is correspondingly exalted, there is hardly a limit to the patient's ability to read, simply from physical indications, the mental states of those who experiment with him.

4. So-called Rapport. This term covers all the facts known, before the subject was scientifically investigated, by such expressions as "personal magnetism," "will power over the subject", etc. It is true that one particular operator alone may be able to hypnotize a particular patient; and in this case the patient is, when hypnotized, open to suggestions from that person only. He is deaf and blind to everything enjoined by anyone else. It is easy to see from what has

already been said that this does not involve any occult nerve influence or mental power. A sensitive patient anybody can hypnotize, provided only that the patient have the idea or conviction that the experimenter possesses such power. Now, let a patient get the idea that only one man can hypnotize him, and that is the beginning of the hypnotic suggestion itself. It is a part of the suggestion that a certain personal Rapport is necessary; so the patient must have this Rapport. This is shown by the fact that when such a patient is hypnotized, the operator en rapport with him can transfer the so-called control to any one else simply by suggesting to the patient that this third party can also hypnotize him. Rapport, therefore, and all the amazing claims of charlatans to powers of charming, stealing another's personality, controlling his will at a distance--all such claims are explained, so far as they have anything to rest upon, by suggestion under conditions of mental hyperasthesia or exaltation.

I may now add certain practical remarks on the subject.

In general, any method which fixes the attention upon a single stimulus long enough is probably sufficient to produce Hypnosis; but the result is quick and profound in proportion as the patient has the idea that it is going to succeed, i. e., gets the suggestion of sleep. It may be said, therefore, that the elaborate performances, such as passes, rubbings, mysterious incantations, etc., often resorted to, have no physiological effect whatever, and only serve to work in the way of suggestion upon the mind of the subject. In view of this it is probable that any person in normal health can be hypnotized, provided he is not too sceptical of the operator's knowledge and power; and, on the contrary, any one can hypnotize another, provided he do not arouse too great scepticism, and is not himself wavering and clumsy. It is probable, however, that susceptibility varies greatly in degree, and that race exerts an important influence. Thus in Europe the French seem to be most susceptible, and the English and Scandinavians least so. The impression that weak-minded persons are most available is quite mistaken. On the contrary, patients in the insane asylums, idiots, etc., are the most refractory. This is to be expected, from the fact that in these cases power of strong, steady attention is wanting. The only class of pathological cases which seem peculiarly open to the hypnotic influence is that of the hystero-epileptics, whose tendencies are toward extreme suggestibility. Further, one may hypnotize himself--what we have called above Auto-suggestion--especially after having been put into the trance more than once by others. When let alone after being hypnotized, the patient usually passes into a normal sleep and wakes naturally.

It is further evident that frequent hypnotization is very damaging if done by the same operator, since then the patient contracts a habit of responding to the same class of suggestions; and this may influence his normal life. A further danger arises from the possibility that all suggestions have not been removed from the patient's mind before his awaking. Competent scientific observers always make it a point to do this. It is possible also that damaging effects result directly to a man from frequent hypnotizing; and this is in some degree probable, simply from the fact that, while it lasts, the state is abnormal. Consequently, all general exhibitions in public, as well as all individual hypnotizing by amateurs, should be prohibited by law, and the whole practical application as well as observation of Hypnosis should be left in the hands of physicians or experts who have proved their fitness by an examination and secured a certificate of licence. In Russia a decree (summer, 1893) permits physicians to practise hypnotism for purposes of cure under official certificates. In France public exhibitions are forbidden.

So-called Criminal Suggestions may be made, with more or less effect, in the hypnotic state. Cases have been tried in the French courts, in which evidence for and against such influence of a third person over the criminal has been admitted. The reality of the phenomenon, however, is in dispute. The Paris school claim that criminal acts may be suggested to the hypnotized subject, which are just as certain to be performed by him as any other acts. Such a subject will discharge a blank-loaded pistol at one, when told to do so, or stab him with a paper dagger. While admitting the facts, the Nancy theorists claim that the subject knows the performance to be a farce; gets suggestions of the unreality of it from the experimenters, and so acquiesces. This is probably true, as is seen in frequent cases in which patients have refused, in hypnotic sleep, to perform suggested acts which shocked their modesty, veracity, etc. This goes to show that the Nancy school are right in saying that while in Hypnosis suggestibility is exaggerated to an enormous degree, still it has limits in the more well-knit habits, moral sentiments, social opinions, etc., of the subject. And it further shows that Hypnosis is probably, as they claim, a temporary disturbance, rather than a pathological condition of mind or body.

There have been many remarkable and sensational cases of cure of disease by hypnotic suggestion, reported especially in France. That hysteria in many of its manifestations has been relieved is certainly true; but that any organic, structural disease has ever been cured by hypnotism is unproved. It is not regarded by medical authorities as an agent of much therapeutic value, and is rarely employed; but it is doubtful, in view of the natural prejudice caused by the pretensions of charlatans, whether its merits have been fairly tested. On the European Continent it has been successfully applied in a great variety of cases; and Bernheim has shown that minor nervous troubles, insomnia, migraines, drunkenness, lighter cases of rheumatism, sexual and digestive disorders, together with a host of smaller temporary causes of pain--corns, cricks in back and side, etc.--may be cured or very materially alleviated by suggestions conveyed in the hypnotic state. In many cases such cures are permanently effected with aid from no other remedies. In a number of great city hospitals patients of recognised classes are at once hypnotized, and suggestions of cure made. Li 閣 eault, the founder of the Nancy school, has the credit of having first made use of hypnosis as a remedial agent. It is also becoming more and more recognised as a method of controlling refractory and violent patients in asylums and reformatory institutions. It must be added, however, that psychological theory rather than medical practice is seriously concerning itself with this subject.

Theory.--Two rival theories are held as to the general character of Hypnosis. The Paris school already referred to, led by the late Dr. Charcot, hold that it is a pathological condition which is most readily induced in patients already mentally diseased or having neuropathic tendencies. They claim that the three stages described above are a discovery of great importance. The so-called Nancy school, on the other hand, led by Bernheim, deny the pathological character of Hypnosis altogether, claiming that the hypnotic condition is nothing more than a special form of ordinary sleep brought on artificially by suggestion. Hypnotic suggestion, say they, is only an exaggeration of an influence to which all persons are normally subject. All the variations, stages, curious phenomena, etc., of the Paris school, they claim, can be explained by this "suggestion" hypothesis. The Nancy school must be considered completely victorious apart from some facts which no theory has yet explained.

Hypnotism shows an intimacy of interaction between mind and body to which current psychology is only beginning to do justice; and it is this aspect of the whole matter which should be emphasized in this connection. The hypnotic condition of consciousness may be taken to represent the working of Suggestion most remarkably.

CHAPTER VIII.

THE TRAINING OF THE MIND--EDUCATIONAL PSYCHOLOGY.

A great deal has been said and written about the physical and mental differences shown by the young; and one of the most oft-repeated of all the charges which we hear brought against the current methods of teaching is that all children are treated alike. The point is carried so far that a teacher is judged from the way he has or has not of getting at the children under him as individuals. All this is a move in the right direction; and yet the subject is still so vague that many of the very critics who declaim against the similar treatment which diverse pupils get at school have no clear idea of what is needed; they merely make demands that the treatment shall suit the child. How each child is to be suited, and the inquiry still back of that, what peculiarity it is in this child or that which is to be "suited"--these things are left to settle themselves.

It is my aim in this chapter to indicate some of the variations which are shown by different children; and on the basis of such facts to endeavour to arrive at a more definite idea of what variations of treatment are called for in the several classes into which the children are divided. I shall confine myself at first to those differences which are more hereditary and constitutional.

First Period--Early Childhood.--The first and most comprehensive distinction is that based on the division of the life of man into the two great spheres of reception and action. The "sensory" and the "motor" are becoming the most common descriptive terms of current psychology. We hear all the while of sensory processes, sensory contents, sensory centres, sensory attention, etc.; and, on the other hand, of motor processes, motor centres, motor ataxy, motor attention, motor consciousness, etc. And in the higher reaches of mental function, the same antithesis comes out in the contrast of sensory and motor aphasia, alexia, sensory and motor types of memory and imagination, etc. Indeed the tendency is now strong to think that when we have assigned a given function of consciousness to one or other side of the nervous apparatus, making it either sensory or motor, then our duty to it is done. Be that as it may, there is no doubt that the distinction is throwing great light on the questions of mind which involve also the correlative questions of the nervous system. This is true of all questions of educational psychology.

This first distinction between children--as having general application--is that which I may cover by saying that some are more active, or motile, while others are more passive, or receptive. This is a common enough distinction; but possibly a word or two on its meaning in the constitution of the child may give it more actual value.

The "active" person to the psychologist is one who is very responsive to what we have called Suggestions. Suggestions may be described in most general terms as any and all the influences from outside, from the environment, both physical and personal, which get a lodgment in consciousness and lead to action. A child who is "suggestible" to a high degree shows it in what we call "motility." The suggestions which take hold of him translate themselves very directly into action. He tends to act promptly, quickly, unreflectively, assimilating the newer elements of the suggestions of the environment to the ways of behaviour fixed by his earlier habits. Generally such a person, child or adult, is said to "jump" at conclusions; he is anxious to know in order to act; he acts in some way on all events or suggestions, even when no course of action is explicitly suggested, and even when one attempts to keep him from acting.

Psychologically such a person is dominated by habit. And this means that his nervous system sets, either by its hereditary tendencies or by the undue predominance of certain elements in his education, quickly in the direction of motor discharge. The great channels of readiest out-pouring from the brain into the muscles have become fixed and pervious; it is hard for the processes once started in the sense centres, such as those of sight, hearing, etc., to hold in their energies. They tend to unstable equilibrium in the direction of certain motor combinations, which in their turn represent certain classes of acts. This is habit; and the person of the extreme motor type is always a creature of habit.

Now what is the line of treatment that such a child should have? The necessity for getting an answer to this question is evident from what was said above--i. e., that the very rise of the condition itself is due, apart from heredity, oftener than not to the fact that he has not had proper treatment from his teachers.

The main point for a teacher to have in mind in dealing with such a boy or girl--the impulsive, active one, always responsive, but almost always in error in what he says and does--is that here is a case of habit. Habit is good; indeed, if we should go a little further we should see that all education is the forming of habits; but here, in this case, what we have is not habits, but habit. This child shows a tendency to habit as such: to habits of any and every kind. The first care of the teacher in order to the control of the formation of habits is in some way to bring about a little inertia of habit, so to speak--a short period of organic hesitation, during which the reasons pro and con for each habit may be brought into the consciousness of the child.

The means by which this tendency to crude, inconsiderate action on the part of the child is to be controlled and regulated is one of the most typical questions for the intelligent teacher. Its answer must be different for children of different ages. The one thing to do, in general, however, from the psychologist's point of view, is in some way to bring about greater complications in the motor processes which the child uses most habitually, and with this complication to get greater inhibition along the undesirable lines of his activity. Inhibition is the damming up of the processes for a period, causing some kind of a "setback" of the energies of movement into the sensory centres, or the redistribution of this energy in more varied and less habitual discharges. With older children a rational method is to analyze for them the mistakes they have made, showing the penalties they have brought upon themselves by hasty action. This requires great watchfulness. In class work, the teacher may profitably point out the better results reached by the pupil who "stops to think." This will bring to the reform of the hasty scholar the added motive of semi-public comparison with the more deliberate members of the class. Such procedure is quite unobjectionable if made a recognised part of the class method; yet care should be taken that no scholar suffer mortification from such comparisons. The matter may be "evened up" by dwelling also on the merit of promptness which the scholar in question will almost always be found to show.

For younger pupils as well as older more indirect methods of treatment are more effective. The teacher should study the scholar to find the general trend of his habits. Then oversight should be exercised over both his tasks and his sports with certain objects in view. His habitual actions should be made as complicated as his ability can cope with; this in order to educate his habits and keep them from working back into mere mechanism. If he shows his fondness for drawing by marking his desk, see that he has drawing materials at hand and some intelligent tasks in this line to do; not as tasks, but for himself. Encourage him to make progress always, not simply to repeat himself. If he has awkward habits of movement with his hands and feet, try to get him interested in games that exercise these members in regular and skilful ways.

Furthermore, in his intellectual tasks such a pupil should be trained, as far as may be, on the more abstract subjects, which do not give immediate openings for action. Mathematics is the best possible discipline for him. Grammar also is good; it serves at once to interest him, if it is well taught, in certain abstract relationships, and also to send out his motor energies in the exercise of speech, which is the function which always needs exercise, and which is always under the observation of the teacher. Grammar, in fact, is one of the very best of primary-school subjects, because instruction in it issues at once in the very motor functions which embody the relationships which the teacher seeks to impress. The teacher has in his ear, so to speak, the evidence as to whether his instruction is understood or not. This gives him a valuable opportunity to keep his instruction well ahead of its motor expression--thus leading the pupil to think rather than to act without thinking--and at the same time to point out the errors of performance which follow from haste in passing from thought to action.

These indirect methods of reaching the impulsive pupil should never be cast aside for the direct effort to "control" such a scholar. The very worst thing that can be done to such a boy or girl is to command him or her to sit still or not to act; and a still worse thing--to make a comparative again on the head of the superlative--is to affix to the command painful penalties. This is a direct violation of the principle of Suggestion. Such a command only tends to empty the pupil's mind of other objects of thought and interest, and so to keep his attention upon his own movements. This, then, amounts to a continual suggestion to him to do just what you want to keep him from doing. On the contrary, unless you give him suggestions and interests which lead his thought away from his acts, it is impossible not to aggravate his bad tendencies by your very efforts. This is the way, as I intimated above, that many teachers create or confirm bad habits in their pupils, and so render any amount of well-intended positive instruction abortive. It seems well established that a suggestion of the negative--that is, not to do a thing--has no negative force; but, on the contrary, in the early period, it amounts only to a stronger suggestion in the positive sense, since it adds emphasis, to the thing which is forbidden. The "not" in a prohibition is no addition to the pictured course to which it is attached, and the physiological fact that the attention tends to set up action upon that which is attended to comes in to put a premium on disobedience. Indeed, the philosophy of all punishment rests in this consideration, i. e., that unless the penalty tends to fill the mind with some object other than the act punished, it does more harm than good. The punishment must be actual and its nature diverting; never a threat which terminates there, nor a penalty which fixes the thought of the offence more strongly in mind. This is to say, that the permanent inhibition of a movement at this period is best secured by establishing some different movement.

The further consideration of the cases of great motility would lead to the examination of the kinds of memory and imagination and their treatment; to that we return below. We may now take up the instances of the sensory type considered with equal generality.

The sensory children are in the main those which seem more passive, more troubled with physical inertia, more contemplative when a little older, less apt in learning to act out new movements, less quick at taking a hint, etc.

These children are generally further distinguished as being--and here the antithesis to the motor ones is very marked--much less suggestible. They seem duller when young. Boys often get credit for dulness compared with girls on this account. Even as early as the second year can this distinction among children be readily observed in many instances. The motor child will show sorrow by loud crying and vigorous action, while the sensory child will grieve in quiet, and continue to grieve when the other has forgotten the disagreeable occurrence altogether. The motor one it is that asks a great many questions and seems to learn little from the answers; while the sensory one learns simply from hearing the questions of the other and the answers given to them. The motor child, again, gets himself hurt a great many times in the same way, without developing enough self-control to restrain himself from the same mistake again and again; the sensory child tends to be timid in the presence of the unknown and uncertain, to learn from one or a few experiences, and to hold back until he gets satisfactory assurances that danger is absent. The former tends to be more restless in sitting, standing, etc., more demonstrative in affection, more impulsive in action, more forgiving in disposition.

As to the treatment of the sensory child, it is a problem of even greater difficulty and danger than that of his motor brother. The very nature of the distinction makes it evident that while the motor individual "gives himself away," so to speak, by constantly acting out his impressions, and so revealing his progress and his errors, with the other it is not so. All knowledge that we are ever able to get of the mental condition of another individual is through his movements, expressive, in a technical sense, or of other kinds, such as his actions, attitudes, lines of conduct, etc. We have no way to read thought directly. So just in so far as the sensory individual is less active, to that degree he is less expressive, less self-revealing. To the teacher, therefore, he is more of an enigma. It is harder to tell in his case what instruction he has appreciated and made his own; and what, on the other hand, has been too hard for him; what wise, and what unwise. Where the child of movement speaks out his impulsive interpretations, this one sinks into himself and gives no answer. So we are deprived of the best way of interpreting him--that afforded by his own interpretation of himself.

A general policy of caution is therefore strongly to be recommended. Let the teacher wait in every case for some positive indication of the child's real state of mind. Even the directions given the child may not have been understood, or the quick word of admonition may have wounded him, or a duty which is so elementary as to be a commonplace in the mental life of the motor child may yet be so vaguely apprehended that to insist upon its direct performance may cost the teacher all his influence with the pupil of this type. It is better to wait even at the apparent risk of losing valuable days than to proceed a single step upon a mistaken estimate of the child's measure of assimilation. And, further, the effect of wrong treatment upon this boy or girl is very different from that of a similar mistake in the other case. He becomes more silent, retired, even secretive, when once an unsympathetic relationship is suggested between him and his elder.

Then more positively--his instruction should be well differentiated. He should in every possible case be given inducements to express himself. Let him recite a great deal. Give him simple verses to repeat. Keep him talking all you can. Show him his mistakes with the utmost deliberation and kindliness of manner; and induce him to repeat his performances in your hearing after the correction has been suggested. Cultivate the imitative tendency in him; it is the handmaid to the formation of facile habits of action. In arranging the children's games, see that he gets the very active parts, even though he be backward and hesitating about assuming them. Make him as far as possible a leader, in order to cultivate his sense of responsibility for the doing of things, and to lead to the expression of his understanding of arrangements, etc. In it all, the essential thing is to bring him out in some kind of expression; both for the sake of the improved balance it gives himself, and as an indication to the observant teacher of his progress and of the next step to be taken in his development.

It is for the sensory child, I think, that the kindergarten has its great utility. It gives him facility in movement and expression, and also some degree of personal and social confidence. But for the same reasons the kindergarten over-stimulates the motor scholars at the corresponding age. There should really be two kindergarten methods--one based on the idea of deliberation, the other on that of expression.

The task of the educator here, it is evident, is to help nature correct a tendency to one-sided development; just as the task is this also in the former case; but here the variation is on the side of idiosyncrasy ultimately, and of genius immediately. For genius, I think, is the more often developed from the contemplative mind, with the relatively dammed-up brain, of this child, than from the smooth-working machine of the motor one. But just for this reason, if the damming-up be liberated, not in the channels of healthy assimilation, and duly correlated growth, but in the forced discharges of violent emotion, followed by conditions of melancholy and by certain unsocial tendencies, then the promise of genius ripens into eccentricity, and the blame is possibly ours.

It seems true--although great caution is necessary in drawing inferences--

that here a certain distinction may be found to hold also between the sexes. It is possible that the apparent precocious alertness of girls in their school years, and earlier, may be simply a predominance among them of the motor individuals. This is borne out by the examination of the kinds of performance in which they seem to be more forward than boys. It resolves itself, so far as my observation goes, into greater quickness of response and greater agility in performance; not greater constructiveness, nor greater power of concentrated attention. The boys seem to need more instruction because they do not learn as much for themselves by acting upon what they already know. In later years, the distinction gets levelled off by the common agencies of education, and by the setting of tasks requiring more thought than the mere spontaneities of either type avail to furnish. Yet all the way through, I think there is something in the ordinary belief that woman is relatively more impulsive and more prone to the less reflective forms of action.

What has now been said may be sufficient to give some concrete force to the common opinion that education should take account of the individual character at this earliest stage. The general distinction between sensory and motor has, however, a higher application in the matter of memory and imagination at later stages of growth, to which we may now turn.

Second Period.--The research is of course more difficult as the pupil grows older, since the influences of heredity tend to become blurred by the more constant elements of the child's home, school, and general social environment. The child whom I described just above as sensory in his type is constantly open to influences from the stimulating behaviour of his motor companion, as well as from the direct measures which parent and teacher take to overcome his too-decided tendencies and to prevent one-sided development. So, too, the motor child tends to find correctives in his environment.

The analogy, however, between the more organic and hereditary differences in individuals, and the intellectual and moral variations which they tend to develop with advance in school age, is very marked; and we find a similar series of distinctions in the later period. The reason that there is a correspondence between the variations given in heredity and those due in the main to the educative influences of the single child's social environment is in itself very suggestive, but space does not permit its exposition here.

The fact is this: the child tends, under the influence of his home, school, social surroundings, etc., to develop a marked character either in the sensory or in the motor direction, in his memory, imagination, and general type of mind.

Taking up the "motor" child first, as before, we find that his psychological growth tends to confirm him in his hereditary type. In all his social dealing with other children he is more or less domineering and self-assertive; or at least his conduct leads one to form that opinion of him. He seems to be constantly impelled to act so as to show himself off. He "performs" before people, shows less modesty than may be thought desirable in one of his tender years, impresses the forms of his own activity upon the other children, who come to stand about him with minds constrained to follow him. He is an object lesson in both the advantages and the risks of an aggressive life policy. He has a suggestion to make in every emergency, a line of conduct for each of his company, all marked out or supplied on the spur of the moment by his own quick sense of appropriate action; and for him, as for no one else, to hesitate is to be lost.

Now what this general policy or method of growth means to his consciousness is becoming more and more clear in the light of the theory of mental types. The reason a person is motor is that his mind tends always to be filled up most easily with memories or revived images of the twitchings, tensions, contractions, expansions, of the activities of the muscular system. He is a motor because the means of his thought generally, the mental coins which pass current in his thought exchange, are muscular sensations or the traces which such sensations have left in his memory. The very means by which he thinks of a situation, an event, a duty, is not the way it looked, or the way it sounded, or the way it smelt, tasted, or felt to the touch--in any of the experiences to which these senses are involved--but the means, the representatives, the instruments of his thought, are the feelings of the way he has acted. He has a tendency--and he comes to have it more and more--to get a muscular representation of everything; and his gauge of the value of this or that is this muscular measure of it, in terms of the action which it is calculated to draw out.

It is then this preference for one particular kind of mental imagery, and that the motor, or muscular kind, which gives this type of child his peculiarity in this more psychological period. When we pass from the mere outward and organic description of his peculiarities, attempted above in the case of very young children, and aim to ascertain the mental peculiarity which accompanies it and carries on the type through the individual's maturer years, we see our way to its meaning. The fact is that a peculiar kind of mental imagery tends to swell up in consciousness and monopolize the theatre of thought. This is only another way of saying that the attention is more or less educated in the direction represented by this sort of imagery. Every time a movement is thought of, in preference to a sound or a sight which is also available, the habit of giving the attention to the muscular equivalents of things becomes more firmly fixed. This continues until the motor habit of attention becomes the only easy and normal way of attending; and then the person is fixed in his type for one, many, or all of his activities of thinking and action.

So now it is no longer difficult to see, I trust, why it is that the child or youth of this sort has the characteristics which he has. It is a familiar principle that attention to the thought of a movement tends to start that very movement. I defy any of my readers to think hard and long of winking the left eye and not have an almost irresistible impulse to wink that eye. There is no better way to make it difficult for a child to sit still than to tell him to sit still; for your words fill up his attention, as I had occasion to say above, with the thought of movements, and these thoughts bring on the movements, despite the best intentions of the child in the way of obedience. Watch an audience of little children--and children of an older growth will also do--when an excited speaker harangues them with many gestures, and see the comical reproduction of the gestures by the children's hands. They picture the movements, the attention is fixed on them, and appropriate actions follow.

It is only the generalizing of these phenomena that we find realized in the boy or girl of the motor type. Such a child is constantly thinking of things by their movement equivalents. Muscular sensations throng up in consciousness at every possible signal and by every train of association; so it is not at all surprising that all informations, instructions, warnings, reproofs, suggestions, pass right through such a child's consciousness and express themselves by the channels of movement. Hence the impulsive, restless, domineering, unmeditative character of the child. We may now endeavour to describe a little more closely his higher mental traits.

1. In the first place the motor mind tends to very quick generalization. Every teacher knows the boys in school who anticipate their conclusions, on the basis of a single illustration. They reach the general notion which is most broad in extent, in application, but most shallow in intent, in richness, in real explaining or descriptive meaning. For example, such a boy will hear the story of Napoleon, proceed to define heroism in terms of military success, and then go out and try the Napoleon act upon his playfellows. This tendency to generalize is the mental counterpart of the tendency to act seen in his conduct. The reason he generalizes is that the brain energies are not held back in the channels of perception, but pour themselves right out toward the motor equivalents of former perceptions which were in any way similar; then the present perceptions are lost in the old ones toward which attention is held by habit, and action follows. To the child all heroes are Napoleons because Napoleon was the first hero, and the channels of action inspired by him suffice now for the appropriate conduct.

2. Such a scholar is very poor at noting and remembering distinctions. This follows naturally from the hasty generalizations which he makes. Having once identified a new fact as the same as an old one, and having so reached a defective sense of the general class, it is then more and more hard for him to retrace his steps and sort out the experiences more carefully. Even when he discovers his mistake, his old impulse to act seizes him again, and he rushes to some new generalization wherewith to replace the old, again falling into error by his stumbling haste to act. The teacher is oftener perhaps brought to the verge of impatience by scholars of this class than by any others.

3. Following, again, from these characteristics, there is a third remark to be made about the youth of this type; and it bears upon a peculiarity which it is very hard for the teacher to estimate and control. These motor boys and girls have what I may characterize as fluidity of the attention. By this is meant a peculiar quality of mind which all experienced teachers are in some degree familiar with, and which they find baffling and unmanageable.

By "fluidity" of the attention I mean the state of hurry, rush, inadequate inspection, quick transition, all-too-ready-assimilation, hear-but-not-heed, in-one-ear-and-out-the-other habit of mind. The best way to get an adequate sense of the state is to recall the pupil who has it to the most marked degree, and picture his mode of dealing with your instructions. Such a pupil hears your words, says "yes," even acts appropriately so far as your immediate instructions go; but when he comes to the same situation again, he is as virginly innocent of your lesson as if his teacher had never been born. Psychologically, the state differs from preoccupation, which characterizes quite a different type of mind. The motor boy is not preoccupied. Far from that, he is quite ready to attend to you. But when he attends, it is with a momentary concentration--with a rush like the flow of a mountain stream past the point of the bank on which you sit. His attention is flowing, always in transition, leaping from "it to that," with superb agility and restlessness. But the exercise it gains from its movements is its only reward. Its acquisitions are slender in the extreme. It illustrates, on the mental plane, the truth of the "rolling stone." It corresponds, as a mental character, to the muscular restlessness which the same type of child shows in the earlier period previously spoken of.

The psychological explanation of this "fluid attention" is more or less plain, but I can not take space to expound it. Suffice it to say that the attention is itself, probably, in its brain seat, a matter of the motor centres; its physical seat both "gives and takes" in co-operation with the processes which shed energy out into the muscles. So it follows that, in the ready muscular revivals, discharges, transitions, which we have seen to be prominent in the motor temperament the attention is carried along, and its "fluidity" is only an incident to the fluidity of the motor symbols of which this sort of a mind continually makes use.

Coming a little closer to the pedagogical problems which this type of pupil raises before us, we find, in the first place, that it is excessively difficult for this scholar to give continuous or adequate attention to anything of any complexity. The movements of attention are so easy, the outlets of energy, to use the physical figure, so large and well used, that the minor relationships of the thing are passed over. The variations of the object from its class are swept away in the onrush of his motor tendencies. He assumes the facts which he does not understand, and goes right on to express himself in action on these assumptions. So while he seems to take in what is told him, with an intuition that is surprisingly swift, and a personal adaptation no less surprising, the disappointment is only the more keen when the instructor finds the next day that he has not penetrated at all into the inner current of this scholar's mental processes.

Again, as marked as this is in its early stages, the continuance of it leads to results which are nothing short of deplorable. When such a student has gone through a preparatory school without overcoming this tendency to "fluid attention" and comes to college, the instructors in the higher institutions are practically helpless before him. We say of him that "he has never learned to study," that he does not know "how to apply himself," that he has no "power of assimilation." All of which simply means that his channels of reaction are so formed already that no instruction can get sufficient lodgment in him to bring about any modification of his "apperceptive systems." The embarrassment is the more marked because such a youth, all through his education period, is willing, ready, evidently receptive, prompt, and punctual in all his tasks.

Now what shall be done with such a student in his early school years? This is a question for the secondary teacher especially, apart from the more primary measures recommended above. It is in the years between eight and fifteen that this type of mind has its rapid development; before that the treatment is mainly preventive, and consists largely in suggestions which aim to make the muscular discharges more deliberate and the general tone less explosive. But when the boy or girl comes to school with the dawning capacity for independent self-direction and personal application, then it is that the problem of the motor scholar becomes critical. The "let-alone" method puts a premium upon the development of his tendencies and the eventual playing out of his mental possibilities in mere motion. Certain positive ways of giving some indirect discipline to the mind of this type may be suggested.

Give this student relatively difficult and complex tasks. There is no way to hinder his exuberant self-discharges except by measures which embarrass and baffle him. We can not "lead him into all truth"; we have to drive him back from all error. The lessons of psychology are to the effect that the normal way to teach caution and deliberation is the way of failure, repulse, and unfortunate, even painful, consequences. Personal appeals to him do little good, since it is a part of his complaint that he is too ready to hear all appeals; and also, since he is not aware of his own lack nor able to carry what he hears into effect. So keep him in company of scholars a little more advanced than he is. Keep him out of the concert recitations, where his tendency to haste would work both personal and social harm. Refrain from giving him assistance in his tasks until he has learned from them something of the real lesson of discouragement, and then help him only by degrees, and by showing him one step at a time, with constant renewals of his own efforts. Shield him with the greatest pains from distractions of all kinds, for even the things and events about him may carry his attention off at the most critical moments. Give him usually the secondary parts in the games of the school, except when real planning, complex execution, and more or less generalship are required; then give him the leading parts: they exercise his activities in new ways not covered by habit, and if he do not rise to their complexity, then the other party to the sport will, and his haste will have its own punishment, and so be a lesson to him.

Besides these general checks and regulations, there remains the very important question as to what studies are most available for this type of mind. I have intimated already the general answer that ought to be given to this question. The aim of the studies of the motor student should be discipline in the direction of correct generalization, and, as helpful to this, discipline in careful observation of concrete facts. On the other hand, the studies which involve principles simply of a descriptive kind should have little place in his daily study. They call out largely the more mechanical operations of memory, and their command can be secured for the most part by mere repetition of details all similar in character and of equal value. The measure of the utility to him of the different studies of the schoolroom is found in the relative demand they make upon him to modify his hasty personal reactions, to suspend his thoughtless rush to general results, and back of it all, to hold the attention long enough upon the facts as they arise to get some sense of the logical relationships which bind them together. Studies which do not afford any logical relationships, and which tend, on the contrary, to foster the habit of learning by repetition, only tend to fix the student in the quality of attention which I have called "fluidity."

In particular, therefore: give this student all the mathematics he can absorb, and pass him from arithmetic into geometry, leaving his algebra till later. Give him plenty of grammar, taught inductively. Start him early in the elements of physics and chemistry. And as opposed to this, keep him out of the classes of descriptive botany and zoology. Rather let him join exploring parties for the study of plants, stones, and animals. A few pet animals are a valuable adjunct to any school museum. If there be an industrial school or machine shop near at hand, try to get him interested in the way things are made, and encourage him to join in such employments. A false generalization in the wheels of a cart supplies its own corrective very quickly, or in the rigging and sails of a toy boat. Drawing from models is a fine exercise for such a youth, and drawing from life, as soon as he gets a little advanced in the control of his pencil. All this, it is easy to see, trains his impulsive movements into some degree of subjection to the deliberative processes.

With this general line of treatment in mind, the details of which the reader will work out in the light of the boy's type, space allows me only two more points before I pass to the sensory scholar.

First, in all the teaching of the type of mind now in question, pursue a method which proceeds from the particular to the general. The discussion of pedagogical method with all its ins and outs needs to take cognizance of the differences of students in their type. The motor student should never, in normal cases, be given a general formula and told to work out particular instances; that is too much his tendency already--to approach facts from the point of view of their resemblances. What he needs rather is a sense of the dignity of the single fact, and of the necessity of giving it its separate place, before hastening on to lose it in the flow of a general statement. So whether the teacher have in hand mathematics, grammar, or science, let him disclose the principles only gradually, and always only so far as they are justified by the observations which the boy has been led to make for himself. For the reason that such a method is practically impossible in the descriptive sciences, and some other branches, as taught in the schoolbooks--botany, zo 鰈 ogy, and, worse than all, history and geography--we should restrict their part in the discipline studies of such a youth. They require simple memory, without observation, and put a premium on hasty and temporary acquisition.

As I have said, algebra should be subordinated to geometry. Algebra has as its distinctive method the principle of substitution, whereby symbols of equal and, for the most part, absolute generality are substituted for one another, and the results stand for one fact as well as for another, in disregard of the worth of the particular in the scheme of nature. For the same reason, deductive logic is not a good discipline for these students; empirical psychology, or political economy, is a better introduction to the moral sciences for them when they reach the high school. This explains what was meant above in the remark as to the method of teaching grammar. As to language study generally, I think the value of it, at this period, and later, is extraordinarily overrated. The proportion of time given to language study in our secondary schools is nothing short of a public crime in its effect upon students of this type--and indeed of any type. This, however, is a matter to which we return below. The average student comes to college with his sense of exploration, his inductive capacity, stifled at its birth. He stands appalled when confronted with the unassimilated details of any science which does not give him a "key" in the shape of general formulas made up beforehand. Were it not that his enlarging experience of life is all the while running counter to the trend of his so-called education, he would probably graduate ready for the social position in which authority takes the place of evidence, and imitation is the method of life.

Second, the teacher should be on the lookout for a tendency which is very characteristic of a student of this type, the tendency, i. e., to fall into elaborate guessing at results. Take a little child of about seven or eight years of age, especially one who has the marks of motor heredity, and observe the method of his acquisition of new words in reading. First he speaks the word which his habit dictates, and, that being wrong, he rolls his eyes away from the text and makes a guess of the first word that comes into his mind; this he keeps up as long as the teacher persists in asking him to try again. Here is the same tendency that carries him later on in his education to a general conclusion by a short cut. He has not learned to interpret the data of a deliberate judgment, and his attention does not dwell on the necessary details. So with him all through his training; he is always ready with a guess. Here, again, the teacher can do him good only by patiently employing the inductive method. Lead him back to the simplest elements of the problem in hand, and help him gradually to build up a result step by step.

I think in this, as in most of the work with these scholars, the association with children of the opposite type is one of the best correctives, provided the companionship is not made altogether one-sided by the motor boy's perpetual monopolizing of all the avenues of personal expression. When he fails in the class, the kind of social lesson which is valuable may be taught him by submitting the same question to a pupil of the plodding, deliberate kind, and waiting for the latter to work it out. Of course, if the teacher have any supervision over the playground, similar treatment can be employed there.

Coming to consider the so-called "sensory" youth of the age between eight, let us say, and sixteen--the age during which the training of the secondary school presents its great problems--we find certain interesting contrasts between this type and that already characterized as "motor." The study of this type of youth is the more pressing for reasons which I have already hinted in considering the same type in the earlier childhood period. It is necessary, first, to endeavour to get a fairly adequate view of the psychological characteristics of this sort of pupil.

The current psychological doctrine of mental "types" rests upon a great mass of facts, drawn in the first instance from the different kinds of mental trouble, especially those which involve derangements of speech--the different kinds of Aphasia. The broadest generalization which is reached from these facts is that which marks the distinction, of which I have already said so much, between the motor and the sensory types. But besides this general distinction there are many finer ones; and in considering the persons of the sensory type, it is necessary to inquire into these finer distinctions. Not only do men and children differ in the matter of the sort of mental material which they find requisite, as to whether it is pictures of movements on the one hand, or pictures from the special senses on the other hand; but they differ also in the latter case with respect to which of the special senses it is, in this case or that, which gives the particular individual his necessary cue, and his most perfect function. So we find inside of the general group called "sensory" several relatively distinct cases, all of which the teacher is likely to come across in varying numbers in a class of pupils. Of these the "visual" and the "auditory" are most important.

There are certain aspects of the case which are so common to all the cases of sensory minds, whether they be visual, auditory, or other, that I may set them out before proceeding further.

First, in all these matters of type distinction, one of the essential things to observe is the behaviour of the Attention. We have already seen that the attention is implicated to a remarkable degree--in what I called "fluid attention" above--in the motor scholar. The same implication of the attention occurs in all the sensory cases, but presents very different aspects; and the common fact that the attention is directly involved affords us one of the best rules of judgment and distinction. We may say, generally, of the sensory children, that the attention is best, most facile, most interest-carrying for some one preferred sense, leading for this sense into preoccupation and ready distraction. This tendency manifests itself, as we saw above, in the motor persons also, taking effect in action, speed, vivacity, hasty generalization, etc.; but in the sensory one it takes on varying forms. This first aspect of our typical distinction of minds we may call "the relation of the 'favoured function' to the attention."

Then, second, there is another and somewhat contrasted relation which also assumes importance when we come to consider individual cases; and that is the relation of the "favoured function"--say movement, vision, hearing, etc.-- to Habit. It is a common enough observation, that habit renders functions easy, and that habits are hard to break; indeed, all treatment of habits is likely to degenerate into the commonplace. But, when looked at as related to the attention, certain truths emerge from the consideration of habit.

In general, we may say that habit bears a twofold relation to attention: on the one hand, facile attention shows the reign of habit. The solid acquisitions are those with which attention is at home, and which are therefore more or less habitual. But, on the other hand, it is equally true that attention is in inverse ratio to habit. We need to attend least to these functions which are most habitual, and we have to attend most to those which are novel and only half acquired. We get new acquisitions mainly, indeed, by strained attention. So we have a contrast of possible interpretations in all cases of sharp and exclusive attention by the children: does the attention represent a Habit in this particular action of the child?--or, does it represent the breaking up of a habit, an act of Accommodation? In each case these questions have to be intelligently considered. The motor person, usually, when uninstructed and not held back, uses his attention under the lead of habit. It is largely the teacher's business in his case, as we saw, to get him to hold, conserve, and direct his attention steadily to the novel and the complex. The sensory person, on the other hand, shows the attention obstructed by details, hindered by novelties, unable to pass smoothly over its acquisitions, and in general lacking the regular influence of habit in leading him to summarize and utilize his mental store in general ways.

The third general aspect of the topic is this: the person of the sensory type is more likely to be the one in whom positive derangement occurs in the higher levels, and in response to the more refined social and personal influences. This, for the reason that this type represents brain processes of greater inertia and complexity, with greater liability to obstruction. They are slower, and proceed over larger brain areas.

With these general remarks, then, on the wider aspects of the distinction of types, we may now turn to one of the particular cases which occurs among sensory individuals. This is all that our space will allow.

The Visual Type.--The so-called "visuals," or "eye-minded" people among us, are numerically the largest class of the sensory population. They resort to visual imagery whenever possible, either because that is the prevailing tendency with them, or because, in the particular function in question in any special act, the visual material comes most readily to mind. The details of fact regarding the "visuals" are very interesting; but I shall not take space to dwell upon them. The sphere in which the facts regarding the pupil of this type are important to the teacher is that of language, taken with the group of problems which arise about instruction in language. The question of his symbolism, and its relations to mathematics, logic, etc., is important. And finally, the sphere of the pupil's expression in all its forms. Then, from all his discoveries in these things, the teacher is called upon to make his method of teaching and his general treatment suitable to this student.

The visual pupil usually shows himself to be so predominately in his speech and language functions; he learns best and fastest from copies which he sees. He delights in illustrations put in terms of vision, as when actually drawn out on the blackboard for him to see. He understands what he reads better than what he hears; and he uses his visual symbols as a sort of common coin into which to convert the images which come to him through his other senses. In regard to the movements of attention, we may say that this boy or girl illustrates both the aspects of the attention-function which I pointed out above; he attends best--that is, most effectively--to visual instruction provided he exert himself; but on the other hand, it is just here that the drift of habit tends to make him superficial. As attention to the visual is the most easy for him, and as the details of his visual stock are most familiar, so he tends to pass too quickly over the new matters which are presented to him, assimilating the details to the old schemes of his habit. It is most important to observe this distinction, since it is analogous to the "fluid attention" of the motor scholar; and some of the very important questions regarding correlation of studies, the training of attention, and the stimulation of interest depend upon its recognition. Acquisition best just where it is most likely to go wrong; that is the state of things. The voluntary use of the visual function gives the best results; but the habitual, involuntary, slipshod use of it gives bad results, and tends to the formation of injurious habits.

For example, I set a strongly visual boy a "copy" to draw. Seeing this visual copy he will quickly recognise it, take it to be very easy, dash it off quickly, all under the lead of habit; but his result is poor, because his habit has taken the place of effort. Once get him to make effort upon it, however, and his will be the best result of all the scholars, perhaps, just because the task calls him out in the line of his favoured function. The same antithesis comes out in connection with other varieties of sensory scholars.

We may say, therefore, in regard to two of the general aspects of mental types--the relation of the favoured function to attention, on the one hand, and to habit, on the other--that they both find emphatic illustration in the pupil of the visual type. He is, more than any other sensory pupil, a special case. His mental processes set decidedly toward vision. He is the more important, also, because he is so common. Statistics are lacking, but possibly half of the entire human family in civilized life are visual in their type for most of the language functions. This is due, no doubt, to the emphasis that civilization puts upon sight as the means of social acquisition generally, and to our predominantly visual methods of instruction.

The third fact mentioned is also illustrated by this type; the fact that mental instruction and derangement may come easily, through the stress laid upon vision in the person's mental economy. I need not enlarge upon the different forms of special defect which come through impairment of sight by central lesion or degeneration of the visual centers and connections. Suffice it to say that they are very common, and very difficult of recovery. The visual person is often so completely a slave to his sight that when that fails either in itself or through weakness of attention he becomes a wreck off the shore of the ocean of intellect. When we consider the large proportion just mentioned of pupils of this type, the care which should be exercised by the school authorities in the matter of favourable conditions of light, avoidance of visual fatigue, proper distance-adjustments in all visual application as regards focus, symmetry, size of objects, copies, prints, etc., becomes at once sufficiently evident to the thoughtful teacher, as it should be still earlier to the parent. There should be a medical examination, by a competent oculist, before the child goes to school, and regular tests afterward. School examiners and boards should have qualifications for reporting on the hygienic conditions of the school as regards lighting. The bright glare of a neighbouring wall before a window toward which children with weak eyes face when at their desks may result not only in common defects of vision but also in resulting mental and moral damage; and the results are worse to those who depend mainly on vision for the food, drink, and exercise, so to speak, of their growing minds.

As to the methods of teaching these and also the other sensory pupils, the indications already given must suffice. The statement of some of these far-reaching problems of educational psychology, and of the directions in which their answers are to be sought, exhausts the purpose of this chapter. In general it may be said that the recommendations made for the treatment of sensory children at the earlier stage may be extended to later periods also, and that the treatment should be, for the most part, in intelligent contrast to that which the motor pupils receive.

Language Study.--From this general consideration of the child's training it becomes evident that the great subjects which are most useful for discipline in the period of secondary education are the mathematical studies on the one hand, which exercise the faculty of abstraction, and the positive sciences, which train the power of observation and require truth to detail. If we should pursue the subject into the collegiate period, we should find mental and moral science, literature, and history coming to their rights. If this be in the main psychological, we see that language study, as such, should have no great place in secondary education. The study of grammar, as has been already said, is very useful in the early periods of development if taught vocally; it brings the child out in self-expression, and carries its own correctives, from the fact that its results are always open to social control. These are, in my mind, the main functions of the study of language.

What, then, is the justification for devoting ten or twelve years of the youth's time to study of a dead language, as is commonly done in the case of Latin? The utility of expression does not enter into it, and the discipline of truth to elegant literary copy can be even so well attained from the study of our own tongue, which is lamentably neglected. In all this dreary language study, the youth's interest is dried up at its source. He is fed on formulas and rules; he has no outlet for invention or discovery; lists of exceptions to the rules destroy the remnant of his curiosity and incentive; even reasoning from analogy is strictly forbidden him; he is shut up from Nature as in a room with no windows; the dictionary is his authority as absolute and final as it is flat and sterile. His very industry, being forced rather than spontaneous, makes him mentally, no less than physically, stoop-shouldered and near-sighted. It seems to be one of those mistakes of the past still so well lodged in tradition and class rivalry that soundness of culture is artificially identified with its maintenance. Yet there is no reason that the spirit of classical culture and the durable elements of Greek and Roman life should not be as well acquired-- nay, better--from the study of history, archeology, and literature. For this language work is not study of literature. Not one in one hundred of the students who are forced through the periodical examinations in these languages ever gets any insight into their aesthetic quality or any inspiration from their form.

But more than this. At least one positively vicious effect follows from language study with grammar and lexicon, no matter what the language be. The habit of intellectual guessing grows with the need of continuous effort in putting together elements which go together for no particular reason. When a thing can not be reasoned out, it may just as well be guessed out. The guess is always easier than the dictionary, and, if successful, it answers just as well. Moreover, the teacher has no way of distinguishing the pupil's replies which are due to the guess from those due to honest work. I venture to say, from personal experience, that no one who has been through the usual classical course in college and before it has not more than once staked his all upon the happy guess at the stubborn author's meaning. This shallow device becomes a substitute for honest struggle. And it is more than shallow; to guess is dishonest. It is a servant to unworthy inertia; and worse, it is a cloak to mental unreadiness and to conscious moral cowardice. The guess is a bluff to fortune when the honest gauntlet of ignorance should be thrown down to the issue.

The effects of this show themselves in a habit of mind tolerated in persons of a literary bent, which is a marked contrast to that demanded and exemplified by science. I think that much of our literary impressionism and sentimentalism reveal the guessing habit.

Yet why guess? Why be content with an impression? Why hint of a "certain this and a certain that" when the "certain," if it mean anything, commonly means the uncertain? Things worth writing about should be formulated clearly enough to be understood. Why let the personal reaction of the individual's feeling suffice? Our youth need to be told that the guess is immoral, that hypothesis is the servant of research, that the private impression instructs nobody, that presentiment is usually wrong, that science is the best antidote to the fear of ghosts, and that the reply "I guess so" betrays itself, whether it arise from bravado, from cowardice, or from literary finesse! I think that the great need of our life is honesty, that the bulwark of honesty in education is exact knowledge with the scientific habit of mind, and, furthermore, that the greatest hindrance to these things is the training which does not, with all the sanctions at its command, distinguish the real, with its infallible tests, from the shadowy and vague, but which contents itself with the throw of the intellectual dice box. Any study which tends to make the difference between truth and error pass with the throwing of a die, and which leads the student to be content with a result he can not verify, has somewhat the function in his education of the puzzle in our society amusements or the game of sliced animals in the nursery.

CHAPTER IX.

THE INDIVIDUAL MIND AND SOCIETY--SOCIAL PSYCHOLOGY.

THE series of questions which arise when we consider the individual as a member of society fall together under the general theory of what has been called, in a figure, Social Heredity.

The treatment of this topic will show something of the normal relation of the individual's mind to the social environment; and the chapter following will give some hints as to the nature and position of that exceptional man in whom we are commonly so much interested--the Genius.

The theory of social heredity has been worked up through the contributions, from different points of view, of several authors. What, then, is social heredity?

This is a very easy question to answer, since the group of facts which the phrase describes are extremely familiar--so much so that the reader may despair, from such a commonplace beginning, of getting any novelty from it. The social heritage is, of course, all that a man or woman gets from the accumulated wisdom of society. All that the ages have handed down--the literature, the art, the habits of social conformity, the experience of social ills, the treatment of crime, the relief of distress, the education of the young, the provision for the old--all, in fact, however described, that we men owe to the ancestors whom we reverence, and to the parents whose presence with us perhaps we cherish still. Their struggles, the orator has told us, have bought our freedom; we enter into the heritage of their thought and wisdom and heroism. All true; we do. We all breathe a social atmosphere; and our growth is by this breathing-in of the tradition and example of the past.

Now, if this be the social heritage, we may go on to ask: Who are to inherit it? To this we may again add the further question: How does the one who is born to such a heritage as this come into his inheritance? And with this yet again: How may he use his inheritance--to what end and under what limitations? These questions come so readily into the mind that we naturally wish the discussion to cover them.

Generally, then, who is eligible for the social inheritance? This heir to society we are, all of us. Society does not make a will, it is true; nor does society die intestate. To say that it is we who inherit the riches of the social past of the race, is to say that we are the children of the past in a sense which comes upon us with all the force that bears in upon the natural heir when he finds his name in will or law. But there are exceptions. And before we seek the marks of the legitimacy of our claim to be the heirs of the hundreds of years of accumulated thought and action, it may be well to advise ourselves as to the poor creatures who do not enter into the inheritance with us. They are those who people our asylums, our reformatories, our jails and penitentiaries; those who prey upon the body of our social life by demands for charitable support, or for the more radical treatment by isolation in institutions; indeed, some who are born to fail in this inheritance are with us no more, even though they were of our generation; they have paid the penalty which their effort to wrest the inheritance from us has cost, and the grave of the murderer, the burglar, the suicide, the red-handed rebel against the law of social inheritance, is now their resting place. Society then is, when taken in the widest sense, made up of two classes of people--the heirs who possess and the delinquents by birth or conduct who have forfeited the inheritance.

We may get a clear idea of the way a man attains his social heritage by dropping figure for the present and speaking in the terms of plain natural science. Ever since Darwin propounded the law of Natural Selection the word Variation has been current in the sense explained on an earlier page.

The student in natural science has come to look for variations as the necessary preliminary to any new step of progress and adaptation in the sphere of organic life. Nature, we now know, is fruitful to an extraordinary degree. She produces many specimens of everything. It is a general fact of reproduction that the offspring of plant or animal is quite out of proportion in numbers to the parents that produce them, and often also to the means of living which await them. One plant produces seeds which are carried far and near--to the ocean and to the desert rocks, no less than to the soil in which they may take root and grow. Insects multiply at a rate which is simply inconceivable to our limited capacity for thinking in figures. Animals also produce more abundantly, and man has children in numbers which allow him to bury half his offspring yearly and yet increase the adult population from year to year. This means, of course, that whatever the inheritance is, all do not inherit it; some must go without a portion whenever the resources of nature, or the family, are in any degree limited and when competition is sharp.

Now Nature solves the problem among the animals in the simplest of ways. All the young born in the same family are not exactly alike; "variations" occur. There are those that are better nourished, those that have larger muscles, those that breathe deeper and run faster. So the question who of these shall inherit the earth, the fields, the air, the water--this is left to itself. The best of all the variations live, and the others die. Those that do live have thus, to all intents and purposes, been "selected" for the inheritance, just as really as if the parents of the species had left a will and had been able to enforce it. This is the principle of "Natural Selection."

Now, this way of looking at problems which involve aggregates of individuals and their distribution is becoming a habit of the age. Wherever the application of the principles of probability do not explain a statistical result-- that is, wherever there seem to be influences which favour particular individuals at the expense of others--men turn at once to the occurrence of Variations for the justification of this seeming partiality of Nature. And what it means is that Nature is partial to individuals in making them, in their natural heredity, rather than after they are born.

The principle of heredity with variations is a safe assumption to make also in regard to mankind; and we see at once that in order to come in for a part in the social heritage of our fathers we must be born fit for it. We must be born so endowed for the race of social life that we assimilate, from our birth up, the spirit of the society into which we are reared. The unfittest, socially, are suppressed. In this there is a distinction between this sphere of survival and that of the animal world. In it the fittest survive, the others are lost; but in society the unfittest are lost, all the others survive. Social selection weeds out the unfit, the murderer, the most unsocial man, and says to him: "You must die"; natural selection seeks out the most fit and says: "You alone are to live." The difference is important, for it marks a prime series of distinctions, when the conceptions drawn from biology are applied to social phenomena; but for the understanding of variations we need not now pursue it further. The contrast may be put, however, in a sentence: in organic evolution we have the natural selection of the fit; in social progress we have the social suppression of the unfit.

Given social variations, therefore, differences among men, what becomes of this man or that? We see at once that if society is to live there must be limits set somewhere to the degree of variation which a given man may show from the standards of society. And we may find out something of these limits by looking at the evident, and marked differences which actually appear about us.

First, there is the idiot. He is not available, from a social point of view, because he varies too much on the side of defect. He shows from infancy that he is unable to enter into the social heritage because he is unable to learn to do social things. His intelligence does not grow with his body. Society pities him if he be without natural protection, and puts him away in an institution. So of the insane, the pronounced lunatic; he varies too much to sustain in any way the wide system of social relationships which society requires of each individual. Either he is unable to take care of himself, or he attempts the life of some one else, or he is the harmless, unsocial thing that wanders among us like an animal or stands in his place like a plant. He is not a factor in social life; he has not come into the inheritance.

Then there is the extraordinary class of people whom we may describe by a stronger term than those already employed. We find not only the unsocial, the negatively unfit, those whom society puts away with pity in its heart; there are also the antisocial, the class whom we usually designate as criminals. These persons, like the others, are variations; but they seem to be variations in quite another way. They do not represent lack on the intellectual side always or alone, but on the moral side, on the social side, as such. The least we can say of the criminals is that they tend, by heredity or by evil example, to violate the rules which society has seen fit to lay down for the general security of men living together in the enjoyment of the social heritage. So far, then, they are factors of disintegration, of destruction; enemies of the social progress which proceeds from generation to generation by just this process of social inheritance. So society says to the criminal also: "You must perish." We kill off the worst, imprison the bad for life, attempt to reform the rest. They, too, then, are excluded from the heritage of the past.

So our lines of eligibility get more and more narrowly drawn. The instances of exclusion now cited serve to give us some insight into the real qualities of the man who lives a social part, and the way he comes to live it.

Passing on to take up the second of the informal topics suggested, we have to find the best description that we can of the social man--the one who is fitted for the social life. This question concerns the process by which any one of us comes into the wealth of relationships which the social life represents. For to say that a man does this is in itself to say that he is the man society is looking for. Indeed, this is the only way to describe the man--to actually find him. Society is essentially a growing, shifting thing. It changes from age to age, from country to country. The Greeks had their social conditions, and the Romans theirs. Even the criminal lines are drawn differently, somewhat, here and there; and in a low stage of civilization a man may pass for normal who, in our time, would be described as weak in mind. This makes it necessary that the standards of judgment of a given society should be determined by an actual examination of the society, and forbids us to say that the limits of variation which society in general will tolerate must be this or that.

We may say, then, that the man who is fit for social life must be born to learn. The need of learning is his essential need. It comes upon him from his birth. Speech is the first great social function which he must learn, and with it all the varieties of verbal accomplishment--reading and writing. This brings to the front the great method of all his learning--imitation. In order to be social he must be imitative, imitative, imitative. He must realize for himself by action the forms, conventions, requirements, co-operations of his social group. All is learning; and learning not by himself and at random, but under the leading of the social conditions which surround him. Plasticity is his safety and the means of his progress. So he grows into the social organization, takes his place as a Socius in the work of the world, and lays deep the sense of values, upon the basis of which his own contributions--if he be destined to make contributions--to the wealth of the world are to be wrought out. This great fact that he is open to the play of the personal influences which are about him is just the "suggestibleness" which we have already described in an earlier chapter; and the influences themselves are "suggestions"--social suggestions. These influences differ in different communities, as we so often remark. The Turk learns to live in a very different system of relations of "give and take" from ours, and ours differ as much from those of the Chinese. All that is characteristic of the race or tribe or group or family--all this sinks into the child and youth by his simple presence there in it, with the capacity to learn by imitation. He is suggestible, and here are the suggestions; he is made to inherit and he inherits. So it makes no difference what his tribe or kindred be; let him be a learner by imitation, and he becomes in turn possessor and teacher.

The case becomes more interesting still when we give the matter another turn, and say that in this learning all the members of society agree; all must be born to learn the same things. They enter, if so be that they do, into the same social inheritance. This again seems like a very commonplace remark; but certain things flow from it. Each member of society gives and gets the same set of social suggestions; the differences being the degree of progress each has made, and the degree of variation which each one gives to what he has before received. This last difference is treated below where we consider the genius.

There grows up, in all this give and take, in all the interchange of suggestions among you, me, and the other, an obscure sense of a certain social understanding about ourselves generally--a Zeitgeist, an atmosphere, a taste, or, in minor matters, a style. It is a very peculiar thing, this social spirit. The best way to understand that you have it, and something of what it is, is to get into a circle in which it is different. The common phrase "fish out of water" is often heard in reference to it. But that does not serve for science. The next best thing that I can do in the way of rendering it is to appeal to another word which has a popular sense, the word Judgment. Let us say that there exists in every society a general system of values, found in social usages, conventions, institutions, and formulas, and that our judgments of social life are founded on our habitual recognition of these values, and of the arrangement of them which has become more or less fixed in our society. For example, to be cordial to a disagreeable neighbour shows good social judgment in a small matter; not to quarrel with the homoeopathic enthusiast who meets you in the street and wishes to doctor your rheumatism out of a symptom book-- that is good judgment. In short, the man gets to show more and more, as he grows up from childhood, a certain good judgment; and his good judgment is also the good judgment of his social set, community, or nation. The psychologist might prefer to say that a man "feels" this; perhaps it would be better for psychological readers to say simply that he has a "sense" of it; but the popular use of the word "judgment" fits so accurately into the line of distinction we are now making that we may adhere to it. So we reach the general position that the eligible candidate for social life must have good judgment as represented by the common standards of judgment of his people.

It may be doubted, however, by some of my readers whether this sense of social values called judgment is the outcome of suggestions operating throughout the term of one's social education. This is an essential point, and I must just assume it. It follows from what we said in an earlier chapter to be the way of the child's learning by imitation. It will appear true, I trust, to any one who may take the pains to observe the child's tentative endeavours to act up to social usages in the family and school. One may then actually see the growth of the sort of judgment which I am describing. Psychologists are coming to see that even the child's sense of his own personal self is a gradual attainment, achieved step by step through his imitative responses to his personal environment. His thought of himself is an interpretation of his thought of others, and his thought of another is doe to further accommodation of his active processes to changes in his thought of a possible self. Around this fundamental movement in his personal growth all the values of his life have their play. So I say that his sense of truth in the social relationships of his environment is the outcome of his very gradual learning of his personal place in these relationships.

We reach the conclusion, therefore, from this part of our study, that the socially unfit person is the person of poor judgment. He may have learned a great deal; he may in the main reproduce the activities required by his social tradition; but with it all he is to a degree out of joint with the general system of estimated values by which society is held together. This may be shown to be true even of the pronounced types of unsocial individuals of whom we had occasion to speak at the outset. The criminal is, socially considered, a man of poor judgment. He may be more than this, it is true. He may have a bad strain of heredity, what the theologians call "original sin"; he then is an "habitual criminal" in the current distinction of criminal types; and his own sense of his failure to accept the teachings of society may be quite absent, since crime is so normal to him. But the fact remains that in his judgment he is mistaken; his normal is not society's normal. He has failed to be educated in the judgments of his fellows, however besides and however more deeply he may have failed. Or, again, the criminal may commit crime simply because he is carried away in an eddy of good companionship, which represents a temporary current of social life; or his nervous energies may be overtaxed temporarily or drained of their strength, so that his education in social judgment is forgotten: he is then the "occasional" criminal. It is true of the man of this type also that while he remains a criminal he has lost his balance, has yielded to temptation, has gratified private impulse at the expense of social sanity; all this shows the lack of that sustaining force of moral consciousness which represents the level of social rightness in his time and place. Then, as to the idiot, the imbecile, the insane, they, too, have no good judgment, for the very adequate but pitiful reason that they have no judgment at all.

This, then, is the doctrine of Social Heredity; it illustrates the side of conformity, of personal acquiescence on the part of the individual in the rules of social life. Another equally important side, that of the personal initiative and influence of the individual mind in society, remains to be spoken of in the next chapter. Social Heredity emphasizes Imitation; the Genius, to whom we now turn, illustrates Invention.

CHAPTER X.

THE GENIUS AND HIS ENVIRONMENT.

The facts concerning the genius seem to indicate that he is a being somewhat exceptional and apart. Common mortals stand about him with expressions of awe. The literature of him is embodied in the alcoves of our libraries most accessible to the public, and even the wayfaring man, to whom life is a weary round, and his conquests over nature and his fellows only the division of honours on a field that usually witnesses drawn battles or bloody defeats, loves to stimulate his courage by hearing of the lives of those who put nature and society so utterly to rout. He hears of men who swayed the destinies of Europe, who taught society by outraging her conventions, whose morality even was reached sometimes by scorn of the peccadilloes which condemn the ordinary man. Every man has in him in some degree the hero worshipper, and gets inflamed somewhat by reading Carlyle's Frederick the Great.

Of course, this popular sense can not be wholly wrong. The genius does accomplish the world movements. Napoleon did set the destiny of Europe, and Frederick did reveal, in a sense, a new phase of moral conduct. The truth of these things is just what makes the enthusiasm of the common man so healthy and stimulating. It is not the least that the genius accomplishes that he thus elevates the traditions of man and inspires the literature that the people read. He sows the seeds of effort in the fertile soil of the newborn of his own kind, while he leads those who do not have the same gifts to rear and tend the growing plant in their own social gardens. This is true; and a philosophy of society should not overlook either of the facts--the actual deeds of the great man with his peculiar influence upon his own time, and his lasting place in the more inspiring social tradition which is embodied in literature and art.

Yet the psychologist has to present just the opposite aspect of these apparent exceptions to the Canons of our ordinary social life. He has to oppose the extreme claim made by the writers who attempt to lift the genius quite out of the normal social movement. For it only needs a moment's consideration to see that if the genius has no reasonable place in the movement of social progress in the world, then there can be no possible doctrine or philosophy of such progress. To the hero worshipper his hero comes in simply to "knock out," so to speak, all the regular movement of the society which is so fortunate, or so unfortunate, as to have given him birth; and by his initiative the aspirations, beliefs, struggles of the community or state get a push in a new direction--a tangent to the former movement or a reversal of it. If this be true, and it be farther true that no genius who is likely to appear can be discounted by any human device before his abrupt appearance upon the stage of action, then the history of facts must take the place of the science or philosophy of them, and the chronicler become the only historian with a right to be.

For of what value can we hold the contribution which the genius makes to thought if this contribution runs so across the acquisitions of the earlier time and the contributions of earlier genius that no line of common truth can be discovered between him and them? Then each society would have its own explanation of itself, and that only so long as it produced no new genius. It may be, of course, that society is so constituted--or, rather, so lacking in constitution--that simple variations in brain physiology are the sufficient reason for its cataclysms; but a great many efforts will be made to prove the contrary before this highest of all spheres of human activity is declared to have no meaning--no thread which runs from age to age and links mankind, the genius and the man who plods, in a common and significant development.

In undertaking this task we must try to judge the genius with reference to the sane social man, the normal Socius. What he is we have seen. He is a person who learns to judge by the judgments of society. What, then, shall we say of the genius from this point of view? Can the hero worshipper be right in saying that the genius teaches society to judge; or shall we say that the genius, like other men, must learn to judge by the judgments of society?

The most fruitful point of view is, no doubt, that which considers the genius a variation. And unless we do this it is evidently impossible to get any theory which will bring him into a general scheme. But how great a variation? And in what direction?--these are the questions. The great variations found in the criminal by heredity, the insane, the idiotic, etc., we have found excluded from society; so we may well ask why the genius is not excluded also. If our determination of the limits within which society decides who is to be excluded is correct, then the genius must come within these limits. He can not escape them and live socially.

The Intelligence of the Genius.--The directions in which the genius actually varies from the average man are evident as a matter of fact. He is, first of all, a man of great power of thought, of great "constructive imagination," as the psychologists say. So let us believe, first, that a genius is a man who has occasionally greater thoughts than other men have. Is this a reason for excluding him from society? Certainly not; for by great thoughts we mean true thoughts, thoughts which will work, thoughts which will bring in a new area in the discovery of principles, or of their application. This is just what all development depends upon, this attainment of novelty, which is consistent with older knowledge and supplementary to it. But suppose a man have thoughts which are not true, which do not fit the topic of their application, which contradict established knowledges, or which result in bizarre and fanciful combinations of them; to that man we deny the name genius; he is a crank, an agitator, an anarchist, or what not. The test, then, which we bring to bear upon the intellectual variations which men show is that of truth, practical workability--in short, to sum it up, "fitness." Any thought, to live and germinate, must be a fit thought. And the community's sense of the fitness of the thought is their rule of judgment.

Now, the way the community got this sense--that is the great result we have reached above. Their sense of fitness is just what I called above their judgment. So far, at least, as it relates to matters of social import, it is of social origin. It reflects the outcome of all social heredity, tradition, education. The sense of social truth is their criterion of social thoughts, and unless the social reformer's thought be in some way fit to go into the setting thus made by earlier social development, he is not a genius but a crank.

I may best show the meaning of the claim that society makes upon the genius by asking in how far in actual life he manages to escape this account of himself to society. The facts are very plain, and this is the class of facts which some writers urge, as supplying an adequate rule for the application of the principles of their social philosophy. The simple fact is, say they, that without the consent of society the thoughts of your hero, whether he be genius or fool, are practically valueless. The fulness of time must come; and the genius before his time, if judged by his works, can not be a genius at all. His thought may be great, so great that, centuries after, society may attain to it as its richest outcome and its profoundest intuition; but before, that time, it is as bizarre as a madman's fancies and as useless. What would be thought, we might be asked by writers of this school, of a rat which developed upon its side the hand of a man, with all its mechanism of bone, muscle, tactile sensibility, and power of delicate manipulation, if the remainder of the creature were true to the pattern of a rat? Would not the rest of the rat tribe be justified in leaving this anomaly behind to starve in the hole where his singular appendage held him fast? Is such a rat any the less a monster because man finds use for his hands.

To a certain extent this argument is forcible and true. If social utility be our rule of definition, then certainly the premature genius is no genius. And this rule of definition may be put in another way which renders it still more plausible. The variations which occur in intellectual endowment, in a community, vary about a mean; there is, theoretically, an average man. The differences among men which can be taken account of in any philosophy of life must be in some way referable to this mean. The variation which does not find its niche at all in the social environment, but which strikes all the social fellows with disapproval, getting no sympathy whatever, is thereby exposed to the charge of being the "sport" of Nature and the fruit of chance. The lack of hearing which awaits such a man sets him in a form of isolation, and stamps him not only as a social crank, but also as a cosmic tramp.

Put in its positive and usual form, this view simply claims that man is always the outcome of the social movement. The reception he gets is a measure of the degree in which he adequately represents this movement. Certain variations are possible--men who are forward in the legitimate progress of society--and these men are the true and only geniuses. Other variations, which seem to discount the future too much, are "sports"; for the only permanent discounting of the future is that which is projected from the elevation of the past.

The great defect of this view is found in its definitions. We exclaim at once: who made the past the measure of the future? and who made social approval the measure of truth? What is there to eclipse the vision of the poet, the inventor, the seer, that he should not see over the heads of his generation, and raise his voice for that which, to all men else, lies behind the veil? The social philosophy of this school can not answer these questions, I think; nor can it meet the appeal we all make to history when we cite the names of Aristotle, Pascal, and Newton, or of any of the men who single-handed and alone have set guide-posts to history, and given to the world large portions of its heritage of truth. What can set limit to the possible variations of fruitful intellectual power? Rare such variations--that is their law: the greater the variation, the more rare! But so is genius; the greater, the more rare. As to the rat with the human hand, he would not be left to starve and decay in his hole; he would be put in alcohol when he died, and kept in a museum! And the lesson which he would teach to the wise biologist would be that here in this rat Nature had shown her genius by discounting in advance the slow processes of evolution!

It is, indeed, the force of such considerations as these which have led to many justifications of the positions that the genius is quite out of connection with the social movement of his time. The genius brings his variations to society whether society will or no; and as to harmony between them, that is a matter of outcome rather than of expectation or theory. We are told the genius comes as a brain-variation; and between the physical heredity which produces him and the social heredity which sets the tradition of his time there is no connection.

But this is not tenable, as we have reason to think, from the interaction which actually takes place between physical and social heredity. To be sure, the heredity of the individual is a physiological matter, in the sense that the son must inherit from his parents and their ancestors alone. But granted that two certain parents are his parents, we may ask how these two certain parents came to be his parents. How did his father come to marry his mother, and the reverse? This is distinctly a social question; and to its solution all the currents of social influence and suggestion contribute. Who is free from social considerations in selecting his wife? Does the coachman have an equal chance to get the heiress, or the blacksmith the clergyman's daughter? Do we find inroads made in Newport society by the ranchman and the dry-goods clerk? And are not the inroads which we do find, the inroads made by the counts and the marquises, due to influences which are quite social and psychological? Again, on the other hand, what leads the count and the marquis, to lay their titles at Newport doors, while the ranchman and the dry-goods clerk keep away, but the ability of both these types of suitors to estimate their chances just on social and psychological grounds? Novelists have rung the changes on this intrusion of social influences into the course of physical heredity. Bourget's Cosmopolis is a picture of the influence of social race characteristics on natural heredity, with the reaction of natural heredity again upon the new social conditions.

A speech of a character of Balzac's is to the point, as illustrating a certain appreciation of these social considerations which we all to a degree entertain. The Duchesse de Carigliano says to Madame de Sommervieux: "I know the world too well, my dear, to abandon myself to the discretion of a too superior man. You should know that one may allow them to court one, but marry them--that is a mistake! Never--no, no. It is like wanting to find pleasure in inspecting the machinery of the opera instead of sitting in a box to enjoy its brilliant illusions." To be sure, we do not generally deliberate in this wise when we fall in love; but that is not necessary, since our social environment sets the style by the kind of intangible deliberation which I have called judgment and fitness. Suppose a large number of Northern advocates of social equality should migrate to the Southern United States, and, true to their theory, intermarry with the blacks. Would it not then be true that a social theory had run athwart the course of physiological descent, leading to the production of a legitimate mulatto society? A new race might spring from such a purely psychological or social initiation.

While not agreeing, therefore, with the theory which makes the genius independent of the social movement--least of all with the doctrine that physical heredity is uninfluenced by social conditions--the hero worshipper is right, nevertheless, in saying that we can not set the limitations of the genius on the side of variations toward high intellectual endowment. So if the general position be true that he is a variation of some kind, we must look elsewhere for the direction of those peculiar traits whose excess would be his condemnation. This we can find only in connection with the other demand that we make of the ordinary man--the demand that he be a man of good judgment. And to this we may now turn.

The Judgment of the Genius.--We should bear in mind in approaching this topic the result which follows from the reciprocal character of social relationships. No genius ever escapes the requirements laid down for his learning, his social heredity. Mentally he is a social outcome, as well as are the fellows who sit in judgment on him. He must judge his own thoughts therefore as they do. And his own proper estimate of things and thoughts, his relative sense of fitness, gets application, by a direct law of his own mental processes, to himself and to his own creations. The limitations which, in the judgment of society, his variations must not overstep, are set by his own judgment also. If the man in question have thoughts which are socially true, he must himself know that they are true. So we reach a conclusion regarding the selection of the particular thoughts which the genius may have: he and society must agree in regard to the fitness of them, although in particular cases this agreement ceases to be the emphatic thing. The essential thing comes to be the reflection of the social standard in the thinker's own judgment; the thoughts thought must always be critically judged by the thinker himself; and for the most part his judgment is at once also the social judgment. This may be illustrated further.

Suppose we take the man of striking thoughts and withal no sense of fitness--none of the judgment about them which society has. He will go through a mighty host of discoveries every hour. The very eccentricity of his imaginations will only appeal to him for the greater admiration. He will bring his most chimerical schemes out and air them with the same assurance with which the real inventor exhibits his. But such a man is not pronounced a genius. If his ravings about this and that are harmless, we smile and let him talk; but if his lack of judgment extend to things of grave import, or be accompanied by equal illusions regarding himself and society in other relationships, then we classify his case and put him into the proper ward for the insane. Two of the commonest forms of such impairment of judgment are seen in the victims of "fixed ideas" on the one hand, and the exalt 闼 on the other. These men have no true sense of values, no way of selecting the fit combinations of imagination from the unfit; and even though some transcendently true and original thought were to flit through the diseased mind of such a one, it would go as it came, and the world would wait for a man with a sense of fitness to arise and rediscover it. The other class, the exalt 闼, are somewhat the reverse; the illusion of personal greatness is so strong that their thoughts seem to them infallible and their persons divine.

Men of such perversions of judgment are common among us. We all know the man who seems to be full of rich and varied thought, who holds us sometimes by the power of his conceptions or the beauty of his creations, but in whose thought we yet find some incongruity, some eminently unfit element, some grotesque application, some elevation or depression from the level of commonplace truth, some ugly strain in the aesthetic impression. The man himself does not know it, and that is the reason he includes it. His sense of fitness is dwarfed or paralyzed. We in the community come to regret that he is so "visionary," with all his talent; so we accommodate ourselves to his unfruitfulness, and at the best only expect an occasional hour's entertainment under the spell of his presence. This certainly is not the man to produce a world movement.

Most of the men we call "cranks" are of this type. They are essentially lacking in judgment, and the popular estimate of them is exactly right.

It is evident, therefore, from this last explanation, that there is a second direction of variation among men: variation in their sense of the truth and value of their own thoughts, and with them of the thoughts of others. This is the great limitation which the man of genius shares with men generally--a limitation in the amount of variation which he may show in his social judgments, especially as these variations affect the claim which he makes upon society for recognition. It is evident that this must be an important factor in our estimate of the claims of the hero to our worship, especially since it is the more obscure side of his temperament, and the side generally overlooked altogether. This let us call, in our further illustrations, the "social sanity" of the man of genius.

The first indication of the kind of social variation which oversteps even the degree of indulgence society is willing to accord to the great thinker is to be found in the effect which education has upon character. The discipline of social development is, as we have seen, mainly conducive to the reduction of eccentricities, the levelling off of personal peculiarities. All who come into the social heritage learn the same great series of lessons derived from the past, and all get the sort of judgment required in social life from the common exercises of the home and school in the formative years of their education. So we should expect that the greater singularities of disposition which represent insuperable difficulty in the process of social assimilation would show themselves early. Here it is that the actual conflict comes--the struggle between impulse and social restraint. Many a genius owes the redemption of his intellectual gifts to legitimate social uses to the victory gained by a teacher and the discipline learned through obedience. And thus it is also that many who give promise of great distinction in early life fail to achieve it. They run off after a phantom, and society pronounces them mad. In their case the personal factor has overcome the social factor; they have failed in the lessons they should have learned, their own self-criticism is undisciplined, and they miss the mark.

These two extremes of variation, however, do not exhaust the case. One of them tends in a measure to the blurring of the light of genius, and the other to the rejection of social restraint to a degree which makes the potential genius over into a crank. The average man is the mean. Put the greatest reach of human attainment, and with it the greatest influence ever exercised by man, is yet more than either of these. It is not enough, the hero worshipper may still say, that the genius should have sane and healthy judgment, as society reckons sanity. The fact still remains that even in his social judgments he may instruct society. He may stand alone and, by sheer might, left his fellow-men up to his point of vantage, to their eternal gain and to his eternal praise. Even let it be that he must have self-criticism, the sense of fitness you speak of, that very sense may transcend the vulgar judgment of his fellows. His judgment may be saner than theirs; and as his intellectual creations are great and unique, so may his sense of their truth be full and unique. Wagner led the musical world by his single-minded devotion to the ideas of Wagner; and Darwin had to be true to his sense of truth and to the formulations of his thought, though no man accorded him the right to instruct his generation either in the one or in the other. To be sure, this divine assurance of the man of genius may be counterfeited; the vulgar dreamer often has it. But, nevertheless, when a genius has it, he is not a vulgar dreamer.

This is true, I think, and the explanation of it leads us to the last fruitful application of the doctrine of variations. Just as the intellectual endowment of men may vary within very wide limits, so may the social qualifications of men. There are men who find it their meat to do society service. There are men so naturally born to take the lead in social reform, in executive matters, in organization, in planning our social campaigns for us, that we turn to them as by instinct. They have a kind of insight to which we can only bow. They gain the confidence of men, win the support of women, and excite the acclamations of children. These people are the social geniuses. They seem to anticipate the discipline of social education. They do not need to learn the lessons of the social environment.

Now, such persons undoubtedly represent a variation toward suggestibility of the most delicate and singular kind. They surpass the teachers from whom they learn. It is hard to say that they "learn to judge by the judgments of society." They so judge without seeming to learn, yet they differ from the man whose eccentricities forbid him to learn through the discipline of society. The two are opposite extremes of variation; that seems to me the only possible construction of them. It is the difference between the ice boat which travels faster than the wind and the skater who braves the wind and battles up-current in it. The latter is soon beaten by the opposition; the former outruns its ally. The crank, the eccentric, the enthusiast--all these run counter to sane social judgment; but the genius leads society to his own point of view, and interprets the social movement so accurately, sympathetically, and with such profound insight that his very singularity gives greater relief to his inspiration.

Now let a man combine with this insight--this extraordinary sanity of social judgment--the power of great inventive and constructive thought, and then, at last, we have our genius, our hero, and one that we well may worship! To great thought he adds balance; to originality, judgment. This is the man to start the world movements if we want a single man to start them. For as he thinks profoundly, so he discriminates his thoughts justly, and assigns them values. His fellows judge with him, or learn to judge after him, and they lend to him the motive forces of success--enthusiasm, reward. He may wait for recognition, he may suffer imprisonment, he may be muzzled for thinking his thoughts, he may die and with him the truth to which he gave but silent birth. But the world comes, by its slower progress, to traverse the path in which he wished to lead it; and if so be that his thought was recorded, posterity revives it in regretful sentences on his tomb.

The two things to be emphasized, therefore, on the rational side of the phenomenally great man--I mean on the side of our means of accounting for him in reasonable terms--are these: first, his intellectual originality; and, second, the sanity of his judgment. And it is the variations in this second sort of endowment which give the ground which various writers have for the one-sided views now current in popular literature.

We are told, on the one hand, that the genius is a "degenerate"; on another hand, that he is to be classed with those of "insane" temper; and yet again, that his main characteristic is his readiness to outrage society by performing criminal acts. All these so-called theories rely upon facts--so far as they have any facts to rest upon--which, if space permitted, we might readily estimate from our present point of view. In so far as a really great man busies himself mainly with things that are objective, which are socially and morally neutral--such as electricity, natural history, mechanical theory, with the applications of these--of course, the mental capacity which he possesses is the main thing, and his absorption in these things may lead to a warped sense of the more ideal and refined relationships which are had in view by the writer in quest for degeneracy. It will still be admitted, however, by those who are conversant with the history of science, that the greatest scientific geniuses have been men of profound quietness of life and normal social development. It is to the literary and artistic genius that the seeker after abnormality has to turn; and in this field, again, the facts serve to show their own meaning.

As a general rule, these artistic prodigies do not represent the union of variations which we find in the greatest genius. Such men are often distinctly lacking in power of sustained constructive thought. Their insight is largely what is called intuitive. They have flashes of emotional experience which crystallize into single creations of art. They depend upon "inspiration"--a word which is responsible for much of the overrating of such men, and for a good many of their illusions. Not that they do not perform great feats in the several spheres in which their several "inspirations" come; but with it all they often present the sort of unbalance and fragmentary intellectual endowment which allies them, in particular instances, to the classes of persons whom the theories we are noticing have in view. It is only to be expected that the sharp jutting variation in the emotional and aesthetic realm which the great artist often shows should carry with it irregularities in heredity in other respects. Moreover, the very habit of living by inspiration brings prominently into view any half-hidden peculiarities which he may have in the remark of his associates, and in the conduct of his own social duties. But mark you, I do not discredit the superb art of many examples of the artistic "degenerate," so-called; that would be to brand some of the highest ministrations of genius, to us men, as random and illegitimate, and to consider impure some of our most exalting and intoxicating sources of inspiration. But I do still say that wherein such men move us and instruct us they are in these spheres above all things sane with our own sanity, and wherein they are insane they do discredit to that highest of all offices to which their better gifts make legitimate claim-- the instruction of mankind.

Again one of Balzac's characters hits the nail on the head. "My dear mother," says Augustine, in the Sign of the Cat and Racket, "you judge superior people too severely. If their ideas were the same as other folks they would not be men of genius."

"Very well," replies Madame Guillaume, "then let men of genius stop at home and not get married. What! A man of genius is to make his wife miserable? And because he is a genius it is all right! Genius! genius! It is not so very clever to say black one minute and white the next, as he does, to interrupt other people, to dance such rigs at home, never to let you know which foot you are to stand on, to compel his wife never to be amused unless my lord is in gay spirits, and to be dull when he is dull."

"But his imaginations...."

"What are such imaginations?" Madame Guillaume went on, interrupting her daughter again. "Fine ones are his, my word! What possesses a man, that all on a sudden, without consulting a doctor, he takes it into his head to eat nothing but vegetables? There, get along! if he were not so grossly immoral, he would be fit to shut up in a lunatic asylum."

"O mother, can you believe?"

"Yes, I do believe. I met him in the Champs Elysees. He was on horseback. Well, at one minute he was galloping as hard as he could tear, and then pulled up to a walk. I said to myself at that moment, 'There is a man devoid of judgment!'"

* * * * *

main consideration which this chapter aims to present, that of the responsibility of all men, be they great or be they small, to the same standards of social judgment, and to the same philosophical treatment, is illustrated in the very man to whose genius we owe the principle upon which my remarks are based--Charles Darwin; and it is singularly appropriate that we should also find the history of this very principle, that of variations with the correlative principle of natural selection, furnishing a capital illustration of our inferences. Darwin was, with the single exception of Aristotle, possibly the man with the sanest judgment that the human mind has ever brought to the investigation of nature. He represented, in an exceedingly adequate way, the progress of scientific method up to his day. He was disciplined in all the natural science of his predecessors. His judgment was an epitome of the scientific insight of the ages which culminated then. The time was ripe for just such a great constructive thought as his--ripe, that is, so far as the accumulation of scientific data was concerned. His judgment differed then from the judgment of his scientific contemporaries mainly in that it was sounder and safer than theirs. And with it Darwin was a great constructive thinker. He had the intellectual strength which put the judgment of his time to the strain--everybody's but his own. This is seen in the fact that Darwin was not the first to speculate in the line of his great discovery, nor to reach formulas; but with the others guessing took the place of Induction. The formula was an uncriticised thought. The unwillingness of society to embrace the hypothesis was justified by the same lack of evidence which prevented the thinkers themselves from giving it proof. And if no Darwin had appeared, the problem of evolution would have been left about where it had been left by the speculations of the Greek mind. Darwin reached his conclusion by what that other great scientific genius in England, Newton, described as the essential of discovery, "patient thought"; and having reached it, he had no alternative but to judge it true and pronounce it to the world.

But the principle of variations with natural selection had the reception which shows that good judgment may rise higher than the level of its own social origin. Even yet the principle of Darwin is but a spreading ferment in many spheres of human thought in which it is destined to bring the same revolution that it has worked in the sciences of organic life. And it was not until other men, who had both authority with the public and sufficient information to follow Darwin's thought, seconded his judgment, that his formula began to have currency in scientific circles.

Now we may ask: Does not any theory of man which loses sight of the supreme sanity of Darwin, and with him of Aristotle, and Angelo, and Leonardo, and Newton, and Leibnitz, and Shakespeare, seem weak and paltry? Do not delicacy of sentiment, brilliancy of wit, fineness of rhythmical and aesthetic sense, the beautiful contributions of the talented special performer, sink into something like apologies--something even like profanation of that name to conjure by, the name of genius? And all the more if the profanation is made real by the moral irregularities or the social shortcomings which give some colour of justification to the appellation "degenerate"!

But, on the other hand, why run to the other extreme and make this most supremely human of all men an anomaly, a prodigy, a bolt from the blue, an element of extreme disorder, born to further or to distract the progress of humanity by a chance which no man can estimate? The resources of psychological theory are adequate, as I have endeavoured to show, to the construction of a doctrine of society which is based upon the individual, in all the possibilities of variation which his heredity may bring forth, and which yet does not hide nor veil those heights of human greatness on which the halo of genius is wont to rest. Let us add knowledge to our surprise in the presence of such a man, and respect to our knowledge, and worship, if you please, to our respect, and with it all we then begin to see that because of him the world is the better place for us to live and work in.

We find that, after all, we may be social psychologists and hero worshippers as well. And by being philosophers we have made our worship more an act of tribute to human nature. The heathen who bows in apprehension or awe before the image of an unknown god may be rendering all the worship he knows; but the soul that finds its divinity by knowledge and love has communion of another kind. So the worship which many render to the unexplained, the fantastic, the cataclysmal--this is the awe that is born of ignorance. Given a philosophy that brings the great into touch with the commonplace, that delineates the forces which arise to their highest grandeur only in a man here and there, that enables us to contrast the best in us with the poverty of him, and then we may do intelligent homage. To know that the greatest men of earth are men who think as I do, but deeper, and see the real as I do, but clearer, who work to the goal that I do, but faster, e humanity as I do, but better--that may be an incitement to my ...ity, but it is also an inspiration to my life.

###

t is it about the
~nature of a child —
it's special qualities
sure relations
the ability to quickly flip from
reality to the imaginary landscape